Missing the Action:

The Films of Chuck Norris

Edited by David C. Hayes

Missing the Action: The Films of Chuck Norris

Published in the USA by
BearManor Media
1317 Edgewater Dr. #110
Orlando, FL 32804
www.BearManorMedia.com

Softcover Edition
ISBN-10:
ISBN-13: 979-8-88771-018-1

Printed in the United States of America

Dedicated in loving memory to Kevin Moyers.

Introduction

I believe the first time I was aware of Chuck Norris as 'Chuck Norris,' was during the media build up for *The Octagon* (1980). That would have made me nine-years-old (ish) and it was post *Star Wars*, so I was acutely aware of film and filmmaking at that point. The idea that a real-life martial arts master starred in a film was exciting. We all knew that movies were make-believe, but here we were, on the precipice of adding true danger and expertise into the smoke and mirrors world of Hollywood. I also believed, at that time, that patriots like Dusty Rhodes were defending my country in wrestling rings against dastardly Russians like Ivan Koloff. I believed a lot of things. Still, the mustachioed spin kicker stood out and that definitely made an impression.

Fast forward, much like a VHS tape (remember to adjust your tracking) to 1988 and we now land on *The Hero and the Terror*, starring Mr. Norris, and then things start to really click for me. At seventeen, I am well into my fascination with the horror genre (complete with a subscription to both *Fangoria* and *Gore Zone*) and here we have that same martial arts master that piqued my childish interest now fighting an indestructible monster. This had the elements of Jason Vorhees and Michael Meyers, the characters that dominated my formative years in film, and I was more than ready to get to it. I had not realized the groundwork had been laid by *Silent Rage* (1982) since my parents deftly kept me away from that one, but I was ready to see Chuck Norris battle a boogeyman. What we got, of course, was a bit different. Playing Danny O'Brien, Chuck slipped into a comfort zone role and the unstoppable monster wasn't that unstoppable and there wasn't much viscera to see and… and… I still liked it. Damn him. Something about Chuck Norris was just appealing. I'm not sure what it was, it wasn't the acting chops (the only chops he did not have) or the action (even at this point it was wearing a bit thin), but there was something…

I delved into the Chuck Norris oeuvre after that, revisiting his appearance with Bruce Li (the real first time I saw him without connecting the dots), watching the everyman character really come to life in *Breaker! Breaker!* (1977) and that is when it hit me: Chuck Norris was just like me, or my father, or any random Joe.

Granted, us normal guys weren't world karate champions or movie stars (yet) but there was something about Chuck that resonated and let one think, 'hey, if he can do it, then I can do it.' Not to cause Aristotle any issues, but it's kind of like the cathartic response when watching thrilling and dangerous media. We'll call it the *Chuckthartic* response and that is the feeling you get when you see someone who is so incredibly average doing above average things. The feeling is rooted in the idea that it could be you and, for all intents and purposes, that COULD have been me (with decades of training, large film budgets, and the ability to grow a stellar mustache). That was the key right there. He was just like us. Think about it. If any normal guy is thrust into a movie role, he would be wooden and not really know how to 'act' for the camera. The genius about the Norris films is that he not only realizes that, but he also doubles down on it, really embodying the concept. He used standard social gender ideas from the era, like the idea that young boys are taught that whatever they accomplish in life they should do it by themselves, and the measure of their worth is how they persevere against real or imagined obstacles, etc. We will never know if these were conscious decisions by Mr. Norris and his people or savvy producers that saw the potential, but it worked. It worked well. It worked so well, and Chuck Norris created so many disparate feelings in people around the globe, that we have a book just like this one.

If my theory is holding water to this point, we can examine the polarizing effect that Mr. Norris has had subsequent to his film work. If he is the everyman, then he is susceptible to the same things that every man is, and that includes ideologies. In this volume you will read entries that laud praise upon Mr. Norris, entries that decry his thespianic abilities, and even entries that mention or simply focus on the lasting effects of his version of American patriotism on a national landscape that adores and worships celebrity status. Therein lies my contention: the everyman aspect of Chuck Norris is not limited to the silver screen (big or small). Normal, average, everyday Joes and Janes and whatever generic non-binary names there are can relate to either being that person with an unfortunate ideology (that they, of course do not believe is unfortunate) or having to cope with someone that has an unfortunate ideology. He is us; we are him. He is that average, everyday sort of person talking too loudly on speakerphone at Home Depot and that is why he persists because if he can do it, we all can do it.

After decades of training, the right friends in Hollywood, and, again, a stellar mustache.

–David C. Hayes

The Wrecking Crew (1968)

I had not realized before going into this flick (Chuck Norris' first credited film) that it was the movie that Quentin Tarantino referenced to such a lovely and reflective extent in the amazing film *Once Upon a Time in Hollywood*. So, when the luminous, ultimately tragic figure Sharon Tate showed up onscreen opposite a seemingly (probably unsurprisingly) drunken Dean Martin, my mind wandered to that movie.

Once Upon a Time in Hollywood was a cathartic experience for me as I'm sure it was for many others. NOTE…spoiler alert if you haven't seen that movie…

When I was a kid, for a while I became obsessed with the Manson case and specifically the murder of the pregnant Sharon Tate. My mother bought me a copy of Vincent Bugliosi's book *Helter Skelter* and over the course of a really dark week, I read it cover to cover twice. It disturbed me greatly and I became very sad over the Tate-LaBianca murders (and angry over Manson's alleged Beatles association). I never really got over it and any mention of Tate in particular made me feel a renewed sense of that darkness.

Fast forward to 2019, sitting in a theater with my pal Glen Birdsall, watching QT's take on 1969 Hollywood. Submerged together in the late sixties California atmosphere and the extraordinary cinematography recreating neon Los Angeles in the Summer of Love, every scene dripping with the ethereal feel of HD cameras dropping in via time machine to an era long past.

It tells the story of struggling TV star Rick Dalton (Leo DiCaprio) and his loyal stunt double (Brad Pitt, transcendent in the part) and the way their fictional story interweaves with non-fictional Hollywood. Of course, the knowledge of the impending murders hangs over every scene and builds an underlying tension. I myself was dreading it.

At one point, Tate, played by the multi-talented Margot Robbie, stops by a theater where her film *The Wrecking Crew* (complete with the aforementioned Dean Martin's pre-George Clooney charming smarm) is showing and decides to take in a viewing.

Seeing Tate in the theater so obviously happy (she looks giddy when the crowd reacts appropriately to her onscreen hijinks) just to see herself on the big screen deepens the feeling of impending doom for her character and did make me drop a tear or two. At the time, I thought it might be the only safe respite from her fate and allowed myself a moment to revel in her joy.

A bit later, Pitt's Cliff Booth shows up at Spahn Ranch (home of the Manson Family) and is embroiled in one of the most suspenseful scenes in film history, in my opinion. It's fascinating to see Cliff's interaction with the Manson girls and Tex Watson and using the audience's prior knowledge of what's to come against us, Tarantino crafts a tense and chilling scene and sets the stage for the inevitable showdown. At this point, we aren't REALLY sure what parts Cliff and Rick will play in the recalling of that tragic night, but it's obvious that it will affect them in some capacity.

The Manson Family shows up, and masterfully are shooed away by Rick Dalton. At this point, we think that might be the reason for tying them in; Dalton unknowingly sent them to the Tate house. But no…they burst in a house to find Cliff and his dog waiting and what follows is one of the most hilariously cathartic but gruesome scenes in Hollywood's very history.

The Manson folks are…*disposed* of by Cliff and Rick (and the best dog in the world, Brandy the pit bull), the Hollywood night stars shine down, and the pregnant Sharon Tate, perhaps on the verge of stardom at some future point, lives.

I did drop a few more tears at this point, though a bit guarded since I was sitting with my buddy Glen and didn't want to reveal that inside I was sobbing uncontrollably (although knowing him, I'm certain he was feeling his own type of reflection). For me, it was the PERFECT ending and elevated a film I was already madly in love with to a top 10 all-time favorite of mine.

Once Upon a Time in Hollywood doesn't bring back Sharon Tate or Jay Sebring or the LaBiancas, but it does work as a way to get some of that (unintended?) myth of the Manson Family back under control. After hearing them spoken of in almost glorified tones as some sort of crime anti-heroes (and seeing a Manson poster on the wall of Laurie Strode for some nonsensical reason in Rob Zombie's doomed, gruesome but corny *Halloween* sequel), there is a measured thrill in hearing Brad Pitt's Booth speak to those "scary monsters" in such a mocking tone.

It also brings the comforting feeling that maybe somewhere in an alternate dimension, the Manson Family, who are painted here as being sort of lucky that they picked unsuspected households for victims, found their comeuppance with a different sort of showdown. The victims lived, Sharon had her baby, maybe picked the right role, found stardom, and they lived happily ever after.

But yes, *The Wrecking Crew*. Sigh. Tate is pleasant, of course. Dean is Dean. Our hero Carlos Ray "Chuck" Norris shows up for maybe a minute and a half with a clean shaven babyface and a sort of "Beatles meet Moe Howard" haircut, jumps around a room for a few seconds, takes a super unconvincing kick to the stomach by dazzlin' Dean (paunch in his fifties, but still doing his thing, bless him), and sort of fades off into the Hollywood night with his first role under his belt.

An inauspicious beginning for one of filmdom's most legendary action heroes, to be sure. But as another martial arts icon, Bruce Lee, tells us in *Once Upon a Time in Hollywood*, "Nobody tries to hurt nobody, just who ends up on their butt."

–Paul Counelis

The Way of the Dragon (1972)

The Way of the Dragon is a pretty standard action/kung fu movie story: A Chinese restaurant in Rome is threatened by the Mafia, who want to own it, and want the Chinese out. Their cousin in Hong Kong sends Tang Lung (Bruce Lee) to help. Of course, they're expecting a lawyer to help in their struggle. Starts off with a bit of fun racist humor (insert sarcasm here), with white people suspicious of the Asian dude. Comedic hijinks follow. Tang meets – then beats, then befriends – the restaurant staff. When the baddies show up, Tang beats them all, too. The cousins are unimpressed by a kung fu fighting country bumpkin...until he kicks Mafia ass on their behalf. The action also causes the cousin's niece, Chen, to thaw out toward him. There's plenty more humor, as you can guess.

The tone of the movie is all over the place, like a lot of Hong Kong/Chinese kung fu movies, with an uneven mix of action, drama, and humor. It's whimsical one moment, and deadly serious the next.

The movie's biggest positive is that the movie is set in Rome, and its exterior shots were obviously filmed there, with all its legendary and recognizable landmarks, like the Colosseum. The Colosseum plays a huge part as the scene of the ultimate battle in the movie's finale. The way it's shot, the location ends up becoming almost as much of a character in itself.

I guess I should probably say here that I've never been a huge fan of Bruce Lee. For me, it's pretty much *Enter the Dragon*, and...that's it. Other movies I've seen from him were fine, but I feel like he needed at least a few more films before you could properly assign him action star status. Something a little deeper and (perhaps) more professionally made than these early movies. Sadly, that wasn't to be, obviously. This may get me in trouble, but I think a big part of why he's considered so legendary today is that he did die young, with only a handful of movies under his belt.

Now, the Chuck Norris connection: When Bruce causes too much trouble, the Mafia have no choice but to call in an out-of-town professional martial arts killer to stop him. Enter Chuck as "Colt." In real life, Chuck and Bruce were martial arts pals, and Bruce got him a job as a heavy on the flick, so they could fight each other on film. It was Chuck's big screen debut, and he doesn't disappoint. Unless I miss my guess, it may also be the only time Chuck ever played a villain. Of course, this being Bruce's movie, he comes out the victor in the end. But abiding by Bruce's philosophy, he never takes pleasure in his enemy's death. In fact, he even treats his enemy well in death, covering his corpse with his shirt as a sign of respect.

Norris really only has that relatively small part – a remorseless, unlikable bad guy with only a few lines – in the last 25 minutes of the movie. So, it's not really a "Chuck Norris movie," per se. Colt communicates mostly with his menacing presence, first proving himself top dog among those seeking to take down Tang, and then later during his inevitable climactic battle with Bruce. Seeing Bruce kick Chuck's hairy ass is pretty hilarious, though. In fact, that hairiness ends up working to Bruce's advantage. At one point in the fight, he grabs a handful of Chuck's chest hair to make the bad guy back off. If you've ever torn off a Band-Aid glued to some body hair, you can sympathize with ol' Chucky.

This is the final battle for Tang and the end of the movie, and the Mafia boss ends up arrested, but I can't imagine this could be the end of the characters being harassed. I mean, I know it's silly to try to go into "realism" with a 1970s action flick, but we're talking about Rome here, in Italy. That's pretty much the heart of Mafia territory. The idea that a boss would allow his whole plot to own the restaurant to be ended by one personal kung fu battle between two characters seems kinda laughable. This guy may be one of the weakest Mafia bosses I've ever seen.

Anyway, I say all that about Chuck to say that I don't have much to say about his involvement in the movie, except in very broad commentary on the conflict between the Chinese and white characters.

The angle I noticed with *Way of the Dragon* isn't Chinese characters facing racism and violence from white, Western enemies, which is a pretty common feature of Asian films and kung fu flicks (especially with Chinese characters living in predominantly white geographical areas). I mean, that is in the movie, obviously. The most interesting thing to me is that in the end, the true enemy of the Chinese characters are themselves. The true villain turns out to be the restaurant owner, Chen's uncle. He *wants* the Mafia to take his business, so he can get paid off and go back home to Hong Kong, rich and comfortable. It was his daughter that called for help, not him. He's tired of the struggle, even resorting to murdering his own employees in the end to be done with it. He even tries killing Tang, which – you can guess – doesn't go well for him. There're even a few Chinese men working for the Mafia don, including a fey (in the sense of the gay slur) man who is constantly screwing over the heroic Chinese characters and trying to bring them under the heel of the Mafia, like he is.

The Norris element in *The Way of the Dragon* is pretty minimal, but still check it out for a good time. It's not – at least, not to me – a shining example of kung fu movies, but it is an entertaining flick with some laughs and some great action and fights.

–Kurt Belcher

The Student Teachers (1973)

aka *College Coeds* aka *Self-Service Schoolgirls* aka *The Learning Factor*

This film had four titles, but it is commonly known as *The Student Teachers*. It is a great example of the sexploitation phase of the 1970s. We don't even last two minutes before a woman takes off her robe in front of a window and stretches. It plays almost like a straight pornographic film, where Chuck's role is more of a cameo than a real role. It's also his American debut, as his prior films were either Canadian or made in Hong Kong. Some sources say that Chuck only knew his part in the movie and did not know the quality of the film or the actual plot dealing with all the nudity. When he found out, he was so pissed, he almost rethought the idea of becoming an actor. I am personally glad he didn't, because this would have been a short book.

First the story, if you can call it that, is that three teachers Rachel, Tracey, and Jody struggle to get through to their students. Of course, a couple of them teach courses that deal with the human body. Rachel is a sex ed teacher. Tracey discovers nude photography, and Jody gets involved in drugs. The drugs scene helps inject even more nudity into this film, because someone important also either runs or frequents a strip club. The next scene after that, has a woman walking in on two people having sex. Also, a rampant rapist that doesn't really show up until half-way through, this is a terrible thing to add at that point. It throws the pacing off the whole movie, then again, you don't really watch this movie for the "artistic quality," you watch for the tits and the ass, and I get that. This film does not disappoint in those categories. It does contain a couple of redeeming qualities, but for the most part, this is a film that Chuck would most likely kick off the resume.

The first thing to notice about this film, is just how badly it does not hold up. It was produced by Julie Corman, who is married to Roger

Corman. It looks like it was shot straight to video and the quality is terrible. The acting requires no talent whatsoever, you just need to have a good-looking body. The writing is terrible with scenes spliced in that make no sense nor have any bearing on the plot. There are also scenes featuring women doing gymnastics done in slow motion. That scene, in particular, has one of the worst musical scores ever set to film. The editing of this movie is also sometimes terrible. You have a character get punched in the face and starts to fall back and then instantly switches to face down. How does a mistake like that even happen? Some of what should be horrible assault scenes are comical. The fake slap sounds along with being able to clearly see that the rapist missed the actresses face is indicative of that. This definitely has elements of things that were relevant in the 1970s: racism and wanting to "fight the man" in particular. The dialogue is, of course, dated as all hell, and it contains one of the greatest uses of the word fucker ever put on film; this also happens in the same scene as the great fight scene where a character, all of a sudden, jumps three feet in one of the worst editing jump cuts and then throws a punch. I know we are supposed to be talking about Chuck, and we will, but this "fight scene" should be studied by film classes everywhere to know what the fuck to avoid when making an action film.

There are some, not many, redeeming qualities about the film, such as, its merciful running time of 78 minutes. There is a particularly powerful scene as two Black individuals, one man and one woman, have a thoughtful dialogue about the quality of their education. I wish there was a better movie that this scene could have been a parr of. The film also concludes with one of the funniest shoot-outs ever set to film. People miss each other when they are just feet apart. It was so cheap and so crappy; you can't help but to laugh at what they were trying to do. It also, of course, has Chuck Norris in a small part as a karate instructor.

Chuck's role is a small cameo, it is almost 'blink and you miss it' level. The camera gets good angles of Chuck doing what he does best. The film is of such poor quality, though, it features a sequence where a piece of wood is broken in midair. I can't actually tell if it was Chuck, but his role is so small, I want to give him credit for as much as I can. I watched his scene, if you can even call it that, and I do not hear one audible line of dialogue from him at all. His total screen time probably amounts to less than a minute of this 78-minute film. His wife also makes a cameo in the film as another karate instructor. This has to be one of the worst films, if not, *the* worst film Chuck Norris has ever done. It's hard to hate Chuck for his involvement, if I was given money to show off a skill set for a few hours and be in a movie I would most likely jump at the chance, too. Let this film be a lesson for all actors: do the research into the quality of people that you are going to be working with, it may not be worth it.

–Stephen Kessen

Slaughter in San Francisco (1974)

Oh, boy! Where do I start with this movie? I could simply suggest that it's a Chuck Norris film unlike any other, but that's likely to incite you to watch it and I don't want your resulting trauma on my conscience.

It's about an Asian American cop, not played by Chuck Norris, who seeks revenge for the murder of his African American partner, also not played by Chuck Norris. Oh, but Chuck Norris is the star of the movie, with his very first top billing. He's the villain of the piece, the brutal leader of the gang that kills Officer John Sumner. Oh, and like every other American actor in this film, he's dubbed into English by a voice actor. Yes, you read that correctly!

At this point, Norris had held the world middleweight karate belt for six years but was best known for battling Bruce Lee in *Way of the Dragon*. While his character in that film fought and died with honour, two crucial notes are warranted: he was fighting for the wrong side, and he did so topless but for a forest of body hair. So, when famed Hong Kong production company Golden Harvest, maker of all the best Jackie Chan movies, capitalised on the breakthrough of martial arts flicks in the States by shooting one in San Francisco, they naturally hired Norris to be the bad guy and had him spend most of his screen time proudly displaying his fur.

That kind of made sense in 1974, without our 2020 hindsight (ha!), but not much else in the film does unless you're versed in the logic of Hong Kong cinema.

You should know that good guys have to be really good guys. Officer Don Wong and Officer John Sumner are so happy to be cops that they fondle their badges while driving around San Francisco, laughing as they look for crimes rather than criminals. Of course, when the latter stumbles on a bank robbery and is shot dead for his troubles, the former must pour Coors on his grave and dedicate himself to revenge.

You should know that everyone has to know kung fu, even if they're African American beat cops and corrupt Irish police chiefs. Robert Jones isn't as good as Don Wong, whose character is named for him, but he pretends well and all the kung fu crooks buy it. When these partners interrupt two men attempting to rape a woman, all the chop socky sound effects we know and love suddenly manifest. There wouldn't be as much kung fu fighting in American streets again until *Martial Law* in 1998.

You should know that all cops have to be overtly corrupt except the hero and the rules always work against him. When Sumner is suckered into a trap and beaten up by ten thugs, Wong comes to his rescue and accidentally kills one of them, so must hand in his badge and gun and be locked up. After he's released, he gets a job as a waiter.

You should know that bad guys have to be really bad guys. Chuck Slaughter (I bet that took some brainstorming) first appears in a restaurant, putting out his cigar on former Officer Wong's hand as he pours Norris's coffee. Continuing to silently pour lands him a $500 tip. Slaughter only knows two kinds of people — "those who obey me and those who die"— and he wants to hire Wong into his gang.

And you should know five minutes in exactly how things will end up, because this script could have been written by a teenager following the archetypal template to the letter. Wong is kept busy seeking revenge down a path that, needless to say, leads right to Slaughter's chest hair. Everything is blatant, from the corrupt police chief, who actually beats Wong up when he brings in a crook, to the boss battle during the finalé. Norris even climbs up onto the edge of an ornamental pond just so Wong can kick him into it.

All the other expected components are here too. There's a gorgeous female presence in Sylvia Zhu, played by Sylvia Chang, who was later both Jackie Chans' mother in *Twin Dragons*. There's a crucial clue to be followed outside the law, this time a ripped shirt. There's a naked girl for no reason whatsoever. There's raucous laughter, often more meaningful than actual dialogue. There's outrageous corruption and inappropriately hilarious dialogue, often together; I laughed aloud at a lawyer's "Stop that!" to a corrupt cop trying to murder his client in a police cell and label it suicide. There are bizarre accents across the voice cast; fully half of these corrupt Frisco cops are inexplicably Irish, whether they look it or not. There's even Lam Ching-Ying, the master in the *Mr. Vampire* movies, as a throwaway gang member.

And there's plenty of opportunity for Chuck Norris, by all accounts a genuinely nice person, to attempt in vain to appear haughty, vicious and uncaring. He isn't in this film for as long as his top billing warrants, but he chews up the scenery all he can when he can, whether it's by punching his way through wooden boards or sitting back and shining an apple on his robe while his men are taken down by former Officer Wong, Don Wong doing a decent job as the *Yellow Faced Tiger* of the original title.

He's not as memorable as Chuck Slaughter though, which is a memorable role for Chuck Norris for all the wrong reasons. You have to go way back to see Norris play a bad guy; he can't relish the sheer villainy needed but he has a worthy smug grin. His body hair is at its peak because he trimmed it after this, taking special care to shave his shoulders for future films. And it's the one and only opportunity to see this iconic American actor dubbed into his own language by an unknown voice. It's a must see you ought to avoid!

–Hal CF Astell

Breaker! Breaker! (1977)

CB radios. Corrupt small town authority figures. Kung Fu.

Honestly, if you put in laser guns and Bigfoot, you would have the perfect encapsulation of everything I wanted from a movie in the 1970s.

Breaker, Breaker is not what one might expect from a Chuck Norris movie, especially if one is only familiar with him as a gun-toting, round-house kick executing bad ass. It is, however, exactly what one would expect from the decade that gave us *Smokey and the Bandit, Convoy, Every Which Way But Loose* and any number of other road movies. Unfortunately, *Breaker, Breaker* lacks the humor, charm, and coherent plot of those movies, settling instead of a city set made out of scrap lumber and dirt populated by a bunch of hillbilly redneck characters left over from a movie about cannibals living in the woods.

Did I mention this takes place in California? Texas City, California to be exact. We are introduced to the town and its leader Judge Joshua Trimmings (George Murdock) in the first scene where all of the town-folk are gathered together to celebrate the fact that the town has been given a charter by the state. It quickly turns into a hive of corruption and criminality that can only be brought to justice by someone like Chuck Norris.

Unfortunately, that justice doesn't really come in the way the viewer wants it to. Norris, in his clean shaven pre-scruffy beard and mustache days, plays J.D. Dawes, a trucker who is coming home after a long time in Alaska. He has a joyous reunion with his dirt-bike driving brother Billy (Michael Augenstein). Then Billy goes off on his "first solo run" in Dawes' truck. Billy doesn't look old enough to drive legally, much less have his CDL, but good for him. He's to pick up a load of frozen dinners. Trust me, this will be important later.

The movie cuts between Billy's run and an encounter Dawes have in a diner. The trucker is challenged to an arm-wrestling contest because he's the champion. The arm wrestling devolves into a full-on brawl. Meanwhile Billy has been tricked off of the highway by Sgt Strode (Don Gentry) and Deputy Boles (Ron Cedillos), the law officers of Texas City. They force Billy into town where Trimmings presides over a mockery of a trial. Billy's rig is impounded, and he is sentenced to a $250 fine or 250 days in jail. He attempts to flee by jumping out a window, which does not prove effective.

Dawes' attempts to teach meditation are interrupted by the phone ringing — one of his friends telling him that there is no news on the search for Billy. Why isn't Dawes out looking himself? Don't worry, he soon remedies this by heading off for Texas City in a bright blue van with a raised suspension and eagles airbrushed on the side. On the way into town he is shot at by two rednecks trying to protect their still. You know, the kind of still that they have all over California fifty years after the end of Prohibition.

We see some random abuse performed by the cops, just so we know that they really are the bad guys. Dawes pulls into a mechanic's and meets the local mentally challenged person, Arney (John Di Fusco). He gets a radiator from the giant junk yard, easily four times the size of the actual town. He tries to question the Judge, who is stinking drunk, then pays for but doesn't eat his donut at the restaurant. He runs afoul of the various town-folk, beats up a bunch of them, and escapes with the waitress Arlene (Terry O'Connor).

Dawes returns to town and overhears the monthly meeting of all of the criminal activity that the town is sponsoring. He fights every able bodied man in the town except Judge Trimmings who is high enough on the food chain to get others to do his dirty work. The fights are choreographed by Norris, so they are at least pretty good and feature one spectacular nut-shot. Dawes escapes in his van, which has been fixed despite the fact that Wade (Paul Kawecki) knows that Strode and Boles are after Dawes.

The cops chase Dawes and his van through the dustiest area of California before he escapes by driving up an incline that the cruisers can't handle.

Dawes spends the night with Arlene again. She serves TV dinners for breakfast and Dawes concludes that they must have Billy's load hidden in the junk yard. When he goes back to look for his brother a third time, he vows to come back for her and her son. Seems kind of quick, but hey, this is Chuck Norris, right?

Stuff happens, there's more fighting, there's a helicopter which the town shouldn't be able to afford, and the average viewer might think it's time to give up on this film. How much redneckery can one take? Don't leave, because you don't want to miss the two big pay offs.

Other truckers, hearing that Dawes has been arrested, drive into Texas City and demolish it. They drive through the buildings, chase women and children, and the whole town is set ablaze with awful 70s special effects.

Then Dawes has his final battle… with Boles. Not the Judge, the main antagonist. He gets his comeuppance when a random trucker drives into his house and disturbs his nap. Not Strode, who has been built up and the main henchman. He's knocked off the road when the truckers first drive into town. No, Dawes and Boles square off a couple of times. Dawes is gut shot, Boles abandons his pistol and nightstick for a bottle. Then the two have their final fight in a horse pen while the horse moves as if tied to Dawes marital arts choreography. After Boles is finished, the horse escapes signifying…um, something?

The film ends with a repeat of the dialog of the town charter celebration playing over the ruins of the town which gives entirely the wrong message, making the viewer sad that Texas City has been destroyed.

This film falls just short of being so bad it's good. If you are a Chuck Norris completist I recommend watching the RiffTrax version.

–Michael Cieslak

Good Guys Wear Black (1978)

My two reviews here are of real anomalies in Chuck Norris's filmography: *Slaughter in San Francisco* was a quintessentially Hong Kong martial arts movie rather than an American one and *Good Guys Wear Black* is a very seventies thriller full of that abiding ache to come to terms with the Vietnam War. It seems to me that Norris, having finally become a bona fide leading man in *Breaker! Breaker!*, wanted to exercise his acting chops instead of just kicking people very hard indeed. The catch, of course, is that he's much better at kicking people very hard indeed than he is at acting, especially back in 1978, so recognisable faces like like Dana Andrews, Jim Backus and James Franciscus walk circles around him on that front.

Norris plays Major John T. Booker, the leader of an elite CIA assassination squad called the Black Tigers, who have been a thorn in the Vietnamese side for years. Franciscus plays Conrad Morgan, the Undersecretary of State, who sends them into Vietnam once more, this time during the peace process. The goal is supposedly to retrieve American POWs, none of whom exist, but it's really to walk the squad into a trap because that's the price his Vietnamese counterpart, Kuong Yen, has on signing a peace treaty.

Of course, Booker screws the whole thing up by being so damn good that he makes it out of the trap with at least some of his men, so insert applicable "Chuck Norris Fact" here. He gets them out of the country too, even though the helicopters supposedly tasked with carrying them home naturally don't show. That's how he knows they were set up.

Fast forward five years to Riverside, CA, though, and it's forgotten, or at least put on serious ice. Booker has moved onwards and upwards: we watch him racing a fast car round a track, handing out graded papers to students and driving a cute journalist to dinner in a Porsche with a license plate of BOOKER. He's a college professor studying for his PhD in political science and teaching while he does so, explaining to his students how Vietnam was a terrible idea.

The war comes back to haunt him on the way to dinner, as a tow truck tries to push his Porsche into traffic. Naturally, the driver claims innocence, but an informant alerts the CIA to the news that the Black Tigers are being systematically killed off. In turn, the CIA tells Booker, handing him the current addresses of the three of his men still alive. It's going to be up to him to find them and keep them safe, while simultaneously figuring out who's behind the "accidents".

There is action here, because this is a Chuck Norris movie, but it's pretty skimpy on the ground for a long while. Even when it does happen, it's not in the expected form of kickass karate: it's with snipers and snowmobiles and bombs. As such, I can't highlight any fight for special notice because we don't really get one until Booker figures out who the chief assassin is and we finally get an actual honest to goodness brawl at an airport baggage claim. I guess the only real fight has to be the best one, right?

The cool moments are just that: moments. In particular, Norris delivers two separate flying kicks that are 'must sees' for anyone reading this. One arrives when a killer tries to escape him on a motorbike; he flying kicks her off it. The other is better still; when another killer aims a car at him, he flying kicks him through the goddamn windscreen. That's why we watch Chuck Norris movies, folks! Screw the intrigue.

Sadly, these moments are few and far between. It really is "Missing the Action". Instead of more iconic Chuck Norris demo reel moments, we get a slew of exposition and political manoeuvring. It's Operation Sandstone and the Phoenix Solution, this man coming back from the dead and that one betraying his principles, blackmail victims blackmailing other people and lots of talky, talky "end justifies the means" crap.

And, quite frankly, we don't care, though it's kept at least a little bearable by the presence of Anne Archer as that journalist, who knows far too much and so ends up along for the ride. I found myself caring a lot more about the antique computer that the CIA agent has in his office and the TV that Morgan has in the back of his limo along with the expected bar and gigantic phone. That's a damn cool accessory for 1978 and it goes to show that being nominated for Secretary of State comes with some serious perks. But computers and TVs really aren't what we're supposed to be focusing on in this movie; Anne Archer can only do so much.

Bizarrely, *Good Guys Wear Black* was a big hit. It cost a million to make but grossed over eighteen at the box office and that prompted Norris to follow it up with another thriller, *A Force of One*, though the fact that he plays a karate champion recruited by the cops in that one rather than a military assassin working for the CIA should highlight how many more kicks that one has.

I do wonder why it was such a hit. Maybe the American people really wanted to come to terms with Vietnam in 1978. Maybe they liked *Breaker! Breaker!* and erroneously thought they'd get more of that cheesy but entertaining all-American kickass action. Maybe they simply couldn't resist the title, which is admittedly cool; I wore it for years myself, emblazoned on a Motörhead shirt. Maybe the name of Chuck Norris was becoming enough to sell a movie.

Whatever the reason, it's hardly the worst way I've spent an hour and a half this year but then this year is 2020. It's not bad, to be fair, but I'd watch *Slaughter in San Francisco* again before re-watching this and that was a frickin' disaster.

–Hal CF Astell

A Force of One (1979)

To me, *A Force of One* feels like the first real Chuck Norris movie, even though it was his seventh film, his fourth as the star and his third as the hero. That's because it doesn't just acknowledge that he's a martial artist but actively plays it up within the context of the script. He's Matt Logan and he's both a karate teacher with his own dojo and a karate champion actively defending his title. He joins the main story because the cops are stuck dealing with a karate killer and they're utterly out of their depth.

I rather like this film, even though it's not far from Gene Siskel's description of being "just a poor excuse for a lot of fighting." Some of that fighting is overdone, because we take a few needless breaks from the story to watch Norris in the ring for far longer than we should. The film could have lost ten minutes of Chuck the Champ and still done exactly what it does in its current version, merely with fewer counts for people to get up off the canvas.

I like it because of its focus on martial arts. After the cops realise that they're up against a murderous martial artist — "Maybe it's one of those karate weirdos, like in the movies"—Clu Gulager realises that they need a non-murderous martial artist to help them out. Logan is clearly a good guy, so it doesn't take too much convincing to carve out some of his teaching time and show the boys in blue how to defend themselves. And yeah, they aren't happy about it either, but they change their tune pretty quickly when they realise how useless they are against this sort of attack.

I like it because of its credible romance. One of those boys in blue is actually a girl in blue and Chuck demonstrates some believable chemistry with top credited Jennifer O'Neill, playing Mandy Rust. Sure, she was a much better actor than he was, especially at this point, but he's said himself that he was "ten times better" than in his prior effort, *Good Guys*

Wear Black. This romance doesn't feel shoehorned into the script just to persuade some women to show up to see an action movie; it feels natural and even touching. Of course, their first date is at a fight, because Jerry Sparks is Logan's next championship defence and, even though the two fighters are friends, he's still doing his homework.

I like it because the cops are natural too. They're down to earth folk who happen to have badges and work undercover for the Narcotics Squad and they're the sort of people we want to have badges. They're not heroes in haloes and they're not the enemy in blue. They're stupid sometimes and they're assholes sometimes too but they're good people and they care. They're so obviously influenced by the similarly earthy and almost as ethnically varied characters of *Hill Street Blues* that I was shocked to find that this came out two years before that show started. The script was by Ernest Tidyman, who had written *Shaft* and *The French Connection*, so I guess a lot more things started with him than I'd previously thought.

I like it because the killer's identity isn't too obvious until its revealed, but he gets plenty of opportunity to be villainous. Before we even meet Matt Logan, we follow a couple of cops to their deaths—one experienced officer and one rookie, who somehow becomes less of a rookie every time he gets remembered—in a sporting goods store. They're following a skateboarder who delivers angel dust, and they figure out how it's getting out right before they're attacked by a mysterious kung fu master who's been lurking in the shadows like a ninja. Next thing we know Murph and Johnson are being fished out of the river with their windpipes crushed.

And I like it because the fight choreography is by Chuck and Aaron Norris, as it ought to be. Aaron is Chuck's younger brother, and he was starting out as a stuntman around the time Chuck was getting serious about acting. He doubled for his brother in *Breaker! Breaker!* and *Good Guys Wear Black*, including the famous flying kick through a windshield, but he earned his first credit as a fight choreographer and stunt coordinator here. Maybe that's really him leaping off a Korean restaurant roof in ninja garb to attack his surprised brother.

Not everything is sunshine and roses, of course. The cops should have figured the clues out sooner, for one. They should certainly have seen the bad apple in their barrel a lot sooner too; we certainly do. And the whole angle with Logan's adopted black son, who wants to fight competitively but isn't ready, is a bundle of little clichés wrapped up in a big one. The script really isn't as bad as Tidyman himself suggests, pointing out that he only wrote it to buy his mother a house and calling it his least successful work. I think it may actually play better now than it did in 1979, now that we can see how ahead of the curve it was in some respects, but it was never going to win him another Academy Award.

It ends up where it ought to end up, with a showdown between Chuck Norris and the Karate Killer and it's a decent one, on and off a mountain road, with all the tough moves and gritty detail that *Good Guys Wear Black* couldn't manage. Chuck even has to steal a police car to get from his championship fight to this one, though Mandy jumps in just in time to keep it vaguely legal, and it gets as edgy as that might suggest. It's actually a million-dollar ending, though not in the way you expect; the killer simply throws a million dollars' worth of drugs at Chuck Norris to distract him. And no, of course that didn't work.

–Hal CF Astell

The Octagon (1980)

The Octagon has sentimental value to me, as it's the only real martial artist movie I can say my whole family watched one night long ago in my childhood home, more than likely because of Chuck Norris' mass appeal to the white nuclear family. Though my brothers and I would watch dubbed martial arts movies every Saturday afternoon on good old Channel 33, you couldn't catch my parents or sister dead sitting through one.

It's been four decades now, so I can't remember much, other than it was in our spacious downstairs living room. Mom and Dad probably shared one couch, a couple siblings another, while the rest of us had front row seats on the carpet right in front of our modestly sized color television. I'm going to gamble Mom made us fresh popped corn on the stovetop. Like the ninjas in *The Octagon*, she was quite stealthy at smuggling grenade-sized bags of the homemade treat in her purse through the theater lobby so not to buy five of everything for us kids to snack on.

Throughout the years I would see many Chuck Norris movies, whether with brothers or friends, but again, this one in particular holds a special place in my heart. And just recently I watched it again. As you read this you may not have the comfort of a couch or wall-to-wall carpeting, or Mom's fresh popped corn, but imagine if you will, you're over my house on Friday night, a stomach full of homemade pizza, sitting in front of the TV, and the movie begins...

It opens with a high-contrast image of our man, tragically two first-named Scott James, and a voiceover said in echoing whisper. We know even less going into the movie than we did a minute ago. But no worries. We're just excited it's Rated R, which surely means boobs or gore, both things our curious minds are hoping to see and lots of it, especially since we have my parents' blessing to watch it. We're off to a promising start as a pair of assassins, one in drag, take out some rich guy in a limo. They blast him into Swiss cheese in what I dub the Bloody Baby-Stroller Massacre.

Next, we find ourselves at the ballet, where we meet James' buddy A.J. (Art Hindle) as they discuss hitting on the lead dancer, Nancy (Kim Lankford). James invites Nancy to dinner where the conversation turns to martial arts. Oddly James seems more interested in her brother, one of two characters we will never formally meet yet are repeatedly referred to.

Despite James' lousy flirting he still ends up at Nancy's house and again we hear the whispering. It's in this light (or dark as the power has been cut) we learn that the whispering voice is actually James' inner voice—his Spidey Sense, if you will. It not only warns him of danger but serves as running commentary. With lots of postscripts. And addendums. You're waiting for him to ask "Is there an echo in here? … Echo!"

A group of ninjas attack! Nancy ignores James' advice to stay down and soon becomes Strike 1 of the girls who will die before he can get them in the sack.

The movie immediately ups its cool credits when Lee Van Cleef comes on screen. Sure, at age 9 you have no clue who he is, but later on you'll learn he's the badass of several Spaghetti Westerns and a one-season wonder called The Master. Van Cleef plays McCarn, the leader of an anti-terrorist group. He tells James about the second character we'll never officially meet--Randy--who is now working for him. (SIDE NOTE: I literally had to rewatch this movie four times to learn who the hell Randy is.)

Even though the movie is filled with flashbacks of James from child- to adulthood we won't get one, single flashback of this notorious fight that keeps getting alluded to, or this "Randy" character. We'll piece together a few lines of dialog from various players (including a cameo by future Ghostbuster Ernie Hudson) to learn James apparently knocked Randy's eye out during a martial arts competition, which is why James quit fighting professionally and Randy joined McCarn's men. But don't bother looking for a man with an eye-patch. If we do see him at any point he must have a fake eye.

What we *will* learn through the many flashbacks and voice-overs is that young James (played by Norris offspring, Mike) and Seikura (the younger version played by Brian Tochi) were half-brothers until the Japanese half breaks "the discipline" by being a sore-loser in a competition between the two. From then on they are to be enemies, says teacher/father, Isawa (John Fijioka). It is Seikura, along with aide Katsumo (Yuki Shimoda), that are training ninja to be global terrorists.

What we'll learn from lots of dialogue is that nearly everything and everyone are connected, from dead dancer Nancy being a courier for the terrorist organization her martial arts brother worked for (the assassin in drag?), to pretend broke down driver and second potential love interest Justine (Karen Carlson).

The unintentionally funniest line in the movie is when A.J. gives us a history lesson on ninjas: "Hey wait a minute! They've been outlawed for over 300 years … Those guys used to have to pull a bow for three years before they'd let 'em use an arrow." (SIDE NOTE: Man, I must have spaced in History. Let's see: Christopher Columbus (check), Lost Colony (check), American Revolution (yeah), Civil War (okay) … Nope, no ninjas. I totally would have stayed awake during that chapter.)

Now, what really irks a nine-year-old boy wanting his fill of R-rating, is when your lead guy constantly refuses the advances of the, what is now, second leading lady. She plainly has ulterior motives, and James has too much integrity to lower his guard--at this rate we'll never see boob! She finally gets tired of his rejection and moves on to A.J., who takes the bait. While he possesses initiative in spades, he equally lacks in execution, and Justine picks up on it quick. No matter how much he wants to be, he's just not James.

She tries to talk A.J. out of the mission, but he's determined. She drives the point home with an apples or oranges analogy, which does nothing to help his low self-esteem and only furthers his need to prove himself. He storms off to get in a taxi just as an assassin's blowgun dart takes out Justine. Strike 2. While we really want to feel sorry for James, that means our chances of seeing any skin is getting ever slimmer. So far, this movie has not earned its R rating, and we're fairly disappointed.

But it's not too late. Maybe third leading lady Aura (Carol Bagdasarian) can save the day. We've watched her training to be a terrorist the whole movie, but she recently defected and is seeking James' help. With A.J. on his way to Seikura's operation, James finally realizes what he has to do. McCarn doesn't really know where the base is, but Aura kinda does, and off they go, following A.J.

James and Aura wind up in a hotel in Central America, each in separate beds *I Love Lucy*-style. But after a little pillow talk, we learn the third time (or girl) is the charm for James. Finally! Now hurry! Don't get her killed! We get a side boob shot before the love scene, interrupted with Seikura's untimely weapons demonstration. Now we know why Seikura must die: he ruined what could have been a solid R rating! No mercy!

A.J. gets captured as soon as he reaches his destination, proving he is definitely the proverbial orange of the late Justine's analogy, not the apple.

And now we're in the homestretch. Night has fallen and James shows up to the fortress where we at last see the titular and angular Octagon up close, a small fighting arena inside the much larger fort Seikura resides. James takes out a few men before being captured just long enough for us to formally be introduced to his brother-turned-nemesis Seikura (Tadashi Yamashita). A.J. is not so much as happy to see his friend but pissed off that James has to rescue him. Seikura releases James to run the deadly training course, the finishing line being dead center of the Octagon. Here James will face Seikura's best man and boss ninja, Kyo (Richard Norton), who hisses like a snake with sleep apnea. Did he swallow boiling ramen and permanently destroy his vocal cords? The guy never speaks a line the entire movie.

Both men start evenly matched with katanas. After a short duel Kyo switches out the blade for a pair of sais. A bit more back and forth and James is disarmed. While it shows James is not invincible (like some other martial artist mentioned in a previous book from this publisher) you can often feel the choreography in this, almost like a school play. "When you finish your line I'll say mine." Except in a play like this, forgetting your line could land you up in the hospital if not dead.

Ultimately James defeats Kyo with a warning from A.J. but both suffer for it: Scott gets a shuriken to the shoulder and A.J. gets a visit to the ground floor with a slit throat.

Taking advantage of the moment with a war cry of "Bleeding nasty cowards," the training-weary students rebel against their masters in an all-out battle. Once the fortress is littered with bodies from both sides, James and Seikura finally face off, but it's not nearly as drawn out as he and Kyo's fight, at least as far as screentime is concerned. Judging by the dawning sun, however, we're led to believe the battle has lasted well into the next day, James with katana, Seikura with kanas. You practically blink and it's over. Seikura is dead.

Sure, the scene is shot nice, but other than Aura's smile we get no epilogue. Roll credits and the movie comes to an end.

Sorry man. I know we waited all week to watch this. Anxiously talked about it over lunch how awesome it was going to be, and all we got was one bloody shootout and a lousy (albeit nice) side boob before bedtime? It never entered our naive minds that my Catholic parents screened the movie beforehand to ensure it lacked any material capable of corrupting our young minds.

Huh. With Octagons like this who needs homework? We should have stuck to geometry.

–A. P. Sessler

An Eye for an Eye (1981)

I once had the privilege of interviewing director Steve Carver about his book, *Western Portraits of Great Character Actors: The Unsung Heroes and Villains of the Silver Screen*. Of course, I wanted to chat with him about his movies too, but I kicked the whole interview off with one question: "How cool is Chuck Norris, in real life?"

"He's very cool," was Steve Carver's reply, and as the eighties began, Chuck was missing the mighty moustache that would eventually give way to the bearded Norris that Carver would direct again in *Lone Wolf McQuade*.

But here in this classic revenge tale which sees Norris playing the strong and silent undercover narcotics cop Sean Kane, cool is an understatement. This character becomes the apotheosis of the "man on a mission" after he and his partner Dave Pierce are sold down the river by a snitch named Montoya (Mel Novak, *Game of Death*). This costs Dave (Terry Kiser, *Weekend at Bernie's*) his life. So, there'll be no spending the weekend at his house on the beach.

Chuck oozes vengeance, but after Shaft, that's right, his Captain is played by Richard Roundtree, calls him a reckless man and fails to see how he can continue to defend Chuck's actions against the criminal underworld of San Francisco. Chuck/Cane has no interest in backing down. He quits. Roundtree smiles, though. He knows Chuck is about to go get an eye for an eye.

After a bagpiped funeral and a 21-gun salute where all the cops are in full regalia, except for Chuck, Cane grieves with Dave's family, specifically with his girlfriend Linda (Rosalind Chao, *Mulan* (2020). She's pissed, like Chuck, and feels as though she may be getting closer to exposing the drug ring responsible through investigative reporting.

Chuck, stoic, goes home to chill and workout on his Total Gym till he is slightly dewy, whilst his well-trained dog, Mort, puts his dirty laundry in the hamper for him as Linda calls and tells Cane that she found the evidence she was looking for. Linda doesn't have time to say much because she has the rampaging Professor (Professor Toru Tanaka, *The Running Man*) chasing her ass through subway with some stock cat and mouse stuff that culminates with The Professor HULK SMASHING Herbie. Das Auto. Linda is the 'key' master, and while Chuck was told to wait for him to hook up with her after he takes a nice night-time cruise across the bay, jumps in his Firebird and finally makes it to the scene, Linda has been throttled to death by Tanaka.

Chuck's buddy is still on active duty Tom McCoy (Matt Clark, *Return to Oz*) and meets him at the site on Linda's demise. Mac probes Chuck for any information he might have about who would do such a thing, but Cane is distant. Murder tends to do that to you.

The scene is broken up when Linda's friend, Heather Sullivan (Maggie Cooper, *B.J. and the Bear*) drops by because she left some her things at Linda's place. Cane has McCoy keep him in the loop when Roundtree shows up and tells Cane to take a walk and thinks it's remarkable how well Chuck's shoulder has healed from his last hot encounter. Heather doesn't understand why Linda was killed, but Cane has no time for dilly dallying or a comment for the press because he realises his car is about to be towed. But nobody takes Chuck Norris's car and gets away with!

After Cane gets his car back in pure Norris fashion, he meets back up with McCoy who tells him the report reads like Linda was being chased by a Sherman tank in a suit who has so far managed to remain invisible. But Shaft, the Captain, has taken over the investigation so the whole thing is now a bit like the Wonka factory.

Chuck goes to visit Linda's dad James (Mako, *Sidekicks*) and like that wily Goodfella Ray Liotta he has a suspicious helicopter following him. This leads to an impressive action set piece which sees Mako's house assaulted while he and Chuck fight them off until Roundtree turns up again to tell Chuck he needs to stay out of the case. Following the triad battle, Mako and Chuck move forward together, though Mako really thinks Chuck should meditate more.

As we move toward the end of the slowly unwinding plot which sees Chuck going home and boxing a bit while having flashbacks of Dave's death. Following this, he visits Amanda at the TV station as they chase Linda's clue and get to meet Christopher Lee (man, how cool). Lee is usually the bad guy. He is again in this one, but we don't get to see Christopher Lee cowering before Norris till the final reel. Before that we have Chuck kicking down cops on the take, greasy brothel owners, and a whole ship full of triads that are bringing drugs in for Lee. Richard Roundtree is consistently pissed by Chuck's interference because they are apparently just waiting to spring their major assault on Lee's compound.

They of course don't decide to mount such an operation till Chuck and Amanda finally get it on; Chuck's dog Mort politely closing the door so has master can play that funky music white boy. Amanda gets kidnapped by Lee, Chuck and Mako have fun storming the castle, there some great fight scenes with Mako taking on Tanaka.

Evil is however vanished, Shaft and Norris share a smile, Mako keeps giving Chuck notes on the importance of mind and body being one as Chuck to squeeze a kiss in with Amanda as the credits roll and Chuck walks off into a future of more facial hair and the chance to team up with Mako again in *Sidekicks*. Love *Sidekicks*.

–Kent Hill

Silent Rage (1982)

During the early 1980s genre fans were lucky enough to experience an evolution of two popular subgenres: the slasher film and the martial arts film. We all know, by this time, Chuck Norris spearheaded the popularity of chop-socky film beyond the 42nd street grindhouses to the much more lucrative multiplexes across America with his hit films *Good Guys Wear Black, The Octagon* and *A Force of One*. At the same time, John Carpenter captivated the horror world with the horror classic *Halloween*. Carpenter's hit brought on a multitude of popular copycats such as *The Burning*, *The Prowler* and another genre juggernaut, the *Friday the 13th* series. The creators of the 1982 Columbia Pictures' Chuck Norris vehicle *Silent Rage* decided to make a film that's essentially a hybrid of the two types of films. Does this mash up of the genres work or is it a kick to the cojones of the viewer?

John Kirby (Brian Libby, *The Octagon, Walker: Texas Ranger*) is having a bad fucking day. His battle-axe wife is screaming her lungs out at just about everyone in his house. If his old lady didn't cause enough frustration, Kirby's kids are also foul-mouthed dirty little cretins to boot. For Johnny, this is the absolute worst time to run out of his crazy pills. Kirby's doctor (Ron Silver, *Blue Steel*) reaches out to him while all of this familial madness is going on to calm John's nerves, and sadly it's too little too late. Not before too long our family man has planted an axe into the melons of both his wife and father in-law. Not before long, our hero is on the scene in the form of rugged Sheriff Dan Stevens and looking to capture the much larger Kirby. He does just that, but being the mass of man Kirby is, the brute escapes on foot. A handful of cops finally put his ass down with some deadly force via a shot gun and several bullets from their trusty revolvers.

Soon Kirby's bullet riddled corpse for whatever reason becomes an experiment for a mad doctor played by Brian DePalma regular, William

Finley (*Phantom of the Paradise*). Dr.Vaughn (Finley) has been working on a new concoction that helps heal wounds almost immediately on human flesh. Pumping this regeneration juice into a nearly dead axe murderer seems like a novel idea. Dr. Halman (Silver), Kirby's psychiatrist is not pleased with his patient being used as a human guinea pig as he knows just how dangerous Kirby was as a mere mortal man. Halman really has no choice in the matter as Vaughn is his superior.

While all this Frankenstein fun is going on, Stevens and his partner Charlie (played by the very lumpy Steven Furst, *Animal House*) are doing their thing, fighting bikers and assorted other bad guys who are in the film and specifically casted to suck on Chuck's foot. This is a nice showcase of classic Norris as he plows through a neatly choreographed scene inside a biker bar. Charlie does absolutely nothing to help his partner but ogle some giant biker chick tits. Furst's character is certainly the comic relief and is good for giggle or two.

Possibly the weakest part of *Silent Rage* is the forced relationship angle between Stevens and Dr. Halman's sister in-law, Alison (Toni Kalem). Their montage of love scenes are about as arousing as Shelly Winters wet farting in a bathtub. Chuck's chest hair doesn't even save the awkwardness of these carnal atrocities. As awful as that sounds, it doesn't do that much to the enjoyment of *Silent Rage.*

Ok, back to the fun shit! As you'd expect, with all of this super-juice pumping in Kirby's veins, it's not long before our unstoppable killer escapes from the laboratory, looking to kill just about everyone in his way. I did see some possible "homages" to *Halloween* with the obvious being the unkillable nature of Kirby and the fact that the killer wears a silver track suit. Michael Myers' plain dark blue mechanic's wardrobe has a similar look in its one-piece simplicity. What we get eventually is Stevens playing the role of Sam Loomis as he hunts down Kirby before too many innocent folks perish at his massive banana hands.

The acting is serviceable for just about everyone in the cast. Chuck is Chuck for the most part and Libby is great as the lanky silent killer. He almost looks like a psychotic version of self-help guru Anthony Robbins. Finley does well as our mad scientist looking to create a superhuman no matter what the risk is. Stephen Furst adds a little comic relief, specifically during a scene in which he tells Sheriff Stevens about a pet he accidentally turned into a popsicle. Don't expect stand out performances, but for a low-budget action flick nobody embarrasses themselves

Writer Joseph Fraley followed up on his success of *Good Guys Wear Black* before taking on the writing duties of *Silent Rage*. Fraley had to be a *Halloween* fan as there are several POV scenes of the killer stalking victims. Director Michael Miller came from some unique beginnings with getting his start in exploitation films like *Street Girls* and *Jackson County Jail* to a prolific TV movie director following the success of *Silent Rage*. The movie is shot well with some pretty effective action sequences with the only drawback being the look of the night scenes. It's too dark at times but that drawback on some occasions lend some moodiness to some of the creepy stalking scenes.

Silent Rage is one of the more unique films in Norris' illustrious filmography. Where a couple of his later films, *Hellbound* and *Hero and the Terror* fail with melding the horror and action combo, *Silent Rage* delivers the goods with a generous amount of blood, creepy atmosphere and just enough martial arts ass-kickery to please fans of both genres.

–Jeff Dolniak

Forced Vengeance (1982)

I thought this was a pretty cool movie when I was about 12, but then I also wore parachute pants and shoplifted, so I wouldn't say my judgment at the time was all that great. Do you wanna know how memorable *Forced Vengeance* is? Let me tell you. I watched this movie when I was first given this assignment and took notes. But time passed and other projects pulled me away, so I was not able to write this as quickly as I had hoped to. Skip forward another six weeks and I go to write this. Well, my notes were pretty shoddy as I had written them as additions to the information my memory would have provided immediately after watching the movie. But I couldn't remember much about the movie at all, so I was forced to sit through it again. The second viewing proved to be much more tedious. But you know, I kind of dig this movie even though it's not going to win any awards. (At least not any you'd want to brag about.)

The one super positive thing I can say about *Forced Vengeance* without any hesitation is that it has one of the most amazing opening title sequences I have ever seen. It really does. It's the sort of opening credit sequence James Bond movies can only wish they had. I'm dead serious. The sequence shows a silhouetted Chuck Norris fighting another man against a bright red neon sign. It looks stunning. But then you see some silhouetted women watching the fight and you think, who the hell are they? But you don't care as a viewer because it looks so cool. You think, man, if this movie has the budget for a title sequence as awesome as this, I'm in for a real cinematic treat. But then later when you learn that this opening credit sequence is actually a scene from the film that has just been cut out and tacked on to the beginning, it feels like a bit of a jip and somehow less cool. So, you have to sit through it all over again. But... if you simply watch the opening credit sequence as its own entity in its own YouTube video, you will enjoy it tremendously.

The film features Norris as a cowboy hat wearing modern day tough guy similar to *Justified*'s Raylan Givens (only without the acting chops or badassery of Timothy Olyphant). I'm sure Norris' Josh Randall could totally kick Raylan's ass with a few of those famous Norris roundhouse kicks, but he is far less cool. The most interesting thing about Josh beyond his fighting skills is the fact that he lives on a boat. And who gives a shit? Sonny Crockett did that too and was cooler.

I'm not going to make fun of this movie too much as it's decent as far as Chuck Norris movies go. (This is like saying a beverage is "pretty tasty as far as piss goes.") *Forced Vengeance's* biggest weakness is the same any other Norris film, and that's Norris himself. Norris cannot act to save his life. I've heard his onscreen charisma (or lack thereof) described as being granite-like, and I think that's unfair to granite. What the hell did granite ever do to anybody? Here's the thing: yes, Norris is a world-class fighter who could go toe to toe with just about anyone. But no one watches a movie to see real fights. It would be far more entertaining to watch someone who could actually act and has to use stunt doubles and pretend to fight than it is to watch someone who can fight but can't act. These are staged fights, not real ones, so who gives a shit if Norris can fight? And while he's no doubt a decent man in real life (despite his awful political stances), he is as bland as a meal consisting of cold, clumpy white rice and lukewarm tap water. The late Steve Carver, who directed Norris in *An Eye for an Eye* and *Lone Wolf McQuade*, once described him as being "white bread" and "not much to work with." And Carver didn't mean that as an insult. He loved Norris, but it's an objective truth. Some actors with no acting talent get by on charisma, but not Norris. Norris is a double threat in that he possesses zero acting talent and zero charisma.

Okay, so let's talk about the movie. The script isn't really all that great and features some really shit dialogue that doesn't do Norris any favors. He has some really awful likes. "Hong Kong is like a slap in the face that makes you feel good" is one. Another Norris line that seems pointless and doesn't have much to do with anything is "The greatest man I ever knew was a homosexual." Weird line, but okay, cool. And Norris isn't the only one spewing crappy dialogue. One character says, "You're going to die one piece at a time." I'm sure the screenwriter thought this was a pretty badass line, and I'm sure third graders would agree with him. Another stupid cardboard-acting-ready line is, "Bodies all over the place. You're a real litterer!"

The movie is fairly entertaining and is somehow more than the sum of its parts, but there are some genuinely terrible moments. One is a scene in which Norris' character goes to see Carl (played by Robert Emhardt). While they are talking, Carl eats peanuts throughout the scene. So even as Norris is speaking, we can hear the sound of Carl chomping on those goddamn peanuts. That's just plain sloppy. I've worked on films with a budget that was less than the cost of a Big Mac. Those movies were crappy, and yet the filmmakers still knew enough not to do this. Hell, the peanuts are so prevalent in the scene that they should have received screen billing.

–Andrew J. Rausch

Lone Wolf McQuade (1983)

First off, I feel like I should admit that I'm not much of a Chuck Norris fan. I liked some of his output from the '70s and '80s, but he was never really my teabag. Him being ultra-conservative now doesn't really endear me to him any further. The big exception is – obviously – *Lone Wolf McQuade*. When I was a kid, it seemed like this flick was in constant rotation on cable, and when it appeared, one of my brothers and I had to watch it every time.

Every. Single. Time.

That's no exaggeration. If *Lone Wolf McQuade* was on, we were watching it. Being two very different people – my brother is a practical, mechanically-inclined guy who loves working outdoors, and I am…neither of those things – it was one of the few movies the two of us could watch and enjoy together.

With Walter Hill's equally dusty, sweaty, and testosterone-fueled *Extreme Prejudice* (1987), *Lone Wolf McQuade* was a modern-day cowboy movie (for which my brother and I also have a shared love). The heroes are fighting, gun-toting tough guys. Nothing more. Any attempt to get deeper than that is dismissed by Norris's Texas Ranger 'J.J. McQuade' here, and Nick Nolte's 'Ranger Jack Benteen' in *Extreme Prejudice*. Neither goes in for that touchy-feely crap.

And the inevitable bad guy was a <u>really bad guy</u>. In *McQuade*, that role is filled with flinty-eyed stoicism by the late, great David Carradine. Sure, his 'Wilkes' is a murderous thug, but the real conflict at the heart of his feud with the hero was, of course, a woman.

In the beautiful Barbara Carrera plays Lola. Like Maria Conchita Alonso's 'Sarita' in "Extreme Prejudice", she's fiery, but mostly serves as window-dressing. The women in these movies are there to be protected – and sometimes sexually coveted, not much more. They try to change their men from being so bullheaded stubborn and going off to get killed because of personal honor. Lola starts out with Wilkes, who has money, fame, and lots of pals with lots of guns. But she can't resist J.J., immediately falling in love with his macho high kicks.

Because, of course, as many gunfights as *Lone Wolf McQuade* has, that was always going to take a backseat to martial arts. This *is* a Chuck Norris movie, after all. We get a taste of this early on, when Wilkes does an exhibition at one of his parties, and J.J. is nearly enticed to enter the ring. Carradine of course famously pretended to know kung fu on the eponymous TV show. In real life, Norris undoubtedly could've whipped David's skinny ass. In fact, Norris probably could've beat up David's entire family. All at once.

Predictably, Wilkes is incensed when Lola runs off to live in sin with J.J. When the "Lone Wolf" Ranger pokes his professional law enforcement nose into Wilkes's nefarious criminal dealings, the baddie strikes back, killing some of J.J.'s comrades. J.J.'s daughter is nearly killed by Wilkes's men, when she and her boyfriend stumble onto their operation. J.J. shifts into action. Speaking of shifting, I should mention here that J.J. owns a Dodge with a supercharged engine. It comes in handy, and not just for outrunning federal agents keeping a cautious eye on him throughout the action.

When McQuade is captured by Wilkes, the baddie beats him, actually *burying him in his badass truck*, and leaves him for dead. Being buried alive is no match for J.J. and his Dodge. In perhaps the best scene in the movie, J.J. <u>drives</u> his truck out of the ground and to safety. Not only does it tear itself free of the dirt, I'm pretty sure J.J.'s Dodge works just fine through the rest of the movie. It's as much of a super-truck as J.J. is a super-Ranger (the badass truck is another reason my brother loves it; he's all about badass vehicles).

Wilkes kidnaps J.J.'s daughter <u>and</u> Lola, making a showdown between the two a virtual certainty. Invading Wilkes's compound south of the border,

J.J. and company fight Wilkes's men and get back the hostages. J.J. and Wilkes have their ass and kick it, too. Ranger McQuade wins (shocker!), but Wilkes has his revenge when he accidentally kills Lola while trying to shoot J.J. Wilkes is as broken up about it as the hero, but neither takes long to mourn: While Wilkes tries to escape, J.J. uses a grenade to blow his ass up.

Norris's previous and subsequent output seemed very much in line with the kinds of movies that were going on around him...just not as good. The *Missing in Action* movies (for which this volume is named) were riffs on Stallone's *Rambo* flicks, just tamer. *Good Guys Always Wear Black* and *The Octagon* extended the kung-fu action popularized by Bruce Lee in the 1970s. And *Code of Silence* presaged the gritty martial arts cop movies that would be run into the ground by Steven Seagal.

Lone Wolf McQuade, on the other hand, always seemed to be in a field where it truly was a lone wolf, with very few contemporaries: Modern westerns. Its only real companions were those in Walter Hill's oeuvre, like the above-mentioned *Extreme Prejudice*. These flicks took all the tropes, both good and bad, of classic westerns and transposed them to the present day. Instead of horses, they had trucks. Instead of 'Injuns,' they had urban gangs and Mexican drug dealers. And – in Chuck's case – instead of two-fisted fights, they had martial arts battles.

I also feel the movie is technically better-made than much of Norris's output. Good cinematography, good stunts, and lots of amazing action. (Like that Dodge bursting out of the ground!) Perhaps the only better Norris film may be *Code of Silence*, directed by Andrew Davis, who went on to make classics like Seagal's *Above the Law* and *Under Siege*, and the Harrison Ford/Tommy Lee Jones blockbuster, *The Fugitive*.

If you're looking for a good time, you can do *far* worse than *Lone Wolf McQuade*.

–Kurt Belcher

Missing in Action (1984)

Missing in Action is the first in a trilogy of films. Starring Chuck Norris as James Braddock, it's a story of revenge and rescue. *Missing in Action* is similar to most action movies of the '80s. It's set in Vietnam, the hero is a former military man or POW, and there are lots of guns. Something I always like to look for in movies are a redeeming quality. This is where the idea of my blog looking at leadership principles in film, Reel Leadership, really started. You can find leadership lessons in any movie you watch. Even *Missing in Action*.

Let's dive in and take a look at just a few of the leadership lessons you can take away from this Chuck Norris festival of explosions.

1. Leaders lead the way:

In a scene that isn't too clear, we see Braddock attacking the Vietnamese soldiers that have held him and his soldiers captive. This could be a scene that is a flashback or a dream. It was never made clear. However, Braddock leads the way for his soldiers. He begins by taking out a few bad guys in a hut, then he moves to an elevated platform and takes out more bad guys. The rest of his soldiers follow suit. They take after his lead. Leaders don't sit back in a comfy, ivory tower. Leaders go forth and conquer. Don't think sitting back is what a leader does. They take action.

2. Look people in the eye:

During a governmental investigation into POWs in Vietnam, the Vietnamese government brought in a lineup of witnesses. These witnesses were coerced into giving statements that Braddock had committed crimes.

They had written out their statements and placed them before those present. When Braddock walked past the witnesses, he looked them in the eye. Each witness then lowered their gaze in shame. They couldn't look Braddock in the eye.

You can tell a lot about the people around you by looking them in the eye. If they're ashamed of something they've done, they will look away. They cannot look at you for an extended period of time. Be a leader who looks people in the eye.

3. Count on your team members:

Braddock needed to leave Lun Ta Hotel to track down the missing POWs. He had gone back to the hotel room with Ann Fitzgerald. Ann believed it was going to be a romantic night, but Braddock had a different idea. He went to the hotel's balcony and began to traverse his way down. Ann saw the Vietnamese guards getting closer to Braddock. Thinking quickly, Ann dropped her glass of champagne and distracted the guards.

Ann's distraction gave Braddock time to get around the building and down to the ground. Her work helped save his life. As a leader, you need to be able to count on your team. They are the lifeblood of your organization. You will have to count on them to have your back time and again. Be a leader who can count on their team.

4. Great leaders convince people to join them:

Jack Tucker was one of Braddock's old army buddies. He also was the man with a boat. When Braddock first approached Tucker, Tucker refused to enter Vietnam. He wanted no part of that country. As Braddock and Tucker spent more time together, Braddock subtly worked on getting Tucker to join him. At first, Tucker was only interested in dropping Braddock off. It soon became Tucker going into Vietnam with Braddock. It wound up with Tucker laying down his life for Braddock and the rescued POWs.

Great leaders don't have to say much to get their team to work for the greater good. They lead through example and their example begins to convince their team of what needs to be done. Work on being the example. Show your team what needs to be done and why. They will join you. Be a leader who is able to convince people to join the team.

5. Leaders have to diffuse the situation:

As Braddock entered the Vietnamese jungle, he noticed a tripwire hidden amongst the trees. He had a choice. He could have left the tripwire active or he could choose to set the tripwire off. Braddock chose to set the tripwire off. He activated the trap and a spiked, wooden ball came crashing down. The trap had been sprung. But... there was more. While the trap had been sprung, a dangerous situation had also been diffused. No one would be hurt by the trap in the jungle anymore.

Great leaders know they're walking into challenging situations. These situations will push leaders to their limits. They will also push the people they lead to their limits. As people reach their limits, situations can boil over. This is where the leader steps in. They see the problem and they begin to work on diffusing the situation. Don't let your team members get to the boiling point. You can help diffuse the situation. Be a leader who diffuses situations.

6. Great leaders inspire:

Braddock went to the POW camp to rescue the United States soldiers being held there. Much to his surprise, the soldiers he rescued were not from the United States. They were the Cambodian Black Panthers. Upon their rescue, the leader of the group said they were now going to fight for their freedom. Braddock's actions inspired these people to action.

Your actions will either inspire your team or discourage your team. You have to make a conscious decision to be a leader who inspires. Work on bringing inspiration and hope to your team. Show them what is out there and how they can accomplish it. This is your task! Choose to accept it. Be a leader who inspires their team.

–Joe LaLonde

Missing in Action 2: The Beginning (1985)

The movie opens in 1972 as Col. James Braddock boards a helicopter and heads into a combat zone in Vietnam. The chopper crashes and he is captured and sent to a prison camp run by Vietnamese Col. Yin.Fast forward 10 years, Ronald Reagan is president, Braddock and several other American soldiers are still in the camp, deemed "Missing in Action" by their country.

The camp is in the deep jungle, Yin is abusive and mean to the U.S. soldiers and any of the other slaves who try to help them. The Vietnamese colonel is an Opium dealer, forcing the soldiers to grow the drug so that it can be sold to the French drug runner, Francois.

Early in the movie an Australian journalist wanders into the camp by accident, and is quickly executed once he is found. Yin continually promises to release all of the soldiers if Braddock will admit to being a war criminal on camera so they can use it for propaganda. Braddock continually refuses until one of his men comes down with Malaria and he gives in, with the promise of treatment from Yin. Yin instead murders the soldier, and Braddock vows to escape and take his revenge. Along the way, Capt. David Nester (played by Steven Williams who I best remember from his role on *Supernatural*) turns against his country and his fellow soldiers after losing hope of ever being rescued.

Showing the brutality of Yin seems to be the primary focus of the first two-thirds of the movie, then finishes with Braddock becoming the first person to ever escape alive. Being the hero, he returns to the camp to fight and kill Yin before escaping with as many of the American soldiers as he can. If you like masculinity porn, this movie is for you. It's just that, jumping from torture scene to torture scene with very little in between. However, it is a much stronger movie than the original *Missing in Action*, despite the issues with it being a prequel. As a prequel, there is zero suspense about whether Braddock will survive or even escape (not that there would have been anyway, the star never died in movies back then), but knowing that going in really cuts into any drama or tension that might have been added with the small possibility of him not escaping the camp. That's the sad part here, these movies weren't really written to be a film and prequel/sequel, instead it was just two different scripts that Cannon Films had and slightly altered them to fit the same character for Chuck Norris to play since they had him under contract, and he was a big draw at the time.

Released in 1984 and 1985, the movies were filmed all at once. After they were finished executives at Cannon decided the second chapter had a better chance at succeeding financially and released it first, adding the subtitle "The Beginning" to this movie before pushing it out a year later. *Braddock: Missing in Action III* was released several years later as a last ditch effort to make money off of Norris' name.

It's hard to fault the logic of the movie executives, though, since *Missing in Action: The Beginning* hauled in just shy of $11 million on a $2.4 million budget. It was peanuts next to the original's box office haul of $22.8 million on nearly the same budget. The third cash grab however failed to win back the audience with a larger, though similar, budget of around $3 million, while earning about $6.1 million at the box office.

The reason Norris was willing to work on the first two movies was to honor his brother, Wieland, who was a private in the 101st Airborne Division, and had been killed in June 1970 in Vietnam while on patrol in the defense of Firebase Ripcord. The Vietnam Veterans Memorial officially lists Wieland as a hostile ground casualty, who was shot with small arms fire. He had only been in Vietnam since late April of that year when he was killed.

Unlike the real-life Vietnam, the movie was shot on location on St. Kitt's in the Caribbean and had somewhere between 25 and 40 on-screen deaths (Braddock sometimes only incapacitated his foes, so it's hard to tell exactly). The most shocking deaths involved Braddock and a flamethrower, but my favorite random death was a soldier being thrown down a long distance, only to obviously turn into a test dummy before smashing into the ground.

That death dovetails nicely with my favorite quote from the movie. As Braddock blows up the hut that he had left Yin's broken and battered body in, he says to himself, "And this is for me!" So was that check, Chuck.

–Dave Herndon

Code of Silence (1985)

First off, I feel like I should mention the movie's director. This is only the fourth flick from American filmmaker Andrew Davis. After his early movies – including the excellent hiker survival movie, *The Final Terror* – he moved into big Hollywood moviemaking with *Code of Silence*. Knowing what he made next gives you an idea of what this movie's like. Right after *Code of Silence*, he launched the career of another martial arts tough guy: Steven Seagal's *Above the Law*. He also made another popular Seagal flick, *Under Siege*, as well as *The Fugitive* with Harrison Ford and Tommy Lee Jones, and *Chain Reaction* with Keanu Reeves and Morgan Freeman. He became synonymous with gritty crime and political thrillers.

What strikes me the most about this movie is that it's a *really* solid crime flick. It makes an effort to be a (mostly) down-to-earth story with a believable plot and characters. Even Norris being a karate expert kinda makes sense, as he trains in his downtime around the other cops in his unit. Then he gets his ass kicked by overwhelming numbers in a huge fight scene. Not many of his movies offer a defeated Norris.

Not to mention the very realistic way it treats the "thin blue line." When a fellow cop frames an innocent boy he murdered by mistake, Cusack has no sympathy or support for him. In turn, the rest of the force turns on Cusack. While Cusack is trying to save the life of Diana (Molly Hagan), the teenage daughter of a low-level mob operative, his friends on the force leave him out to dry. To get the job done, Cusack is forced to defy his superiors and steal police armaments – including a brand-new police robot, which must've seemed like science fiction in the mid-1980s. Then again, so many police-themed movies were going this route at the time – see *Blue Thunder* with Roy Scheider and *Runaway* with Tom Selleck for others. Cusack goes rogue to rescue the girl. Seeing police treated as anything other than perfect public servants in an '80s action movie is unheard of – especially in a movie starring the ultraconservative Norris.

That idea of the thin blue line – never rat on a fellow officer – is one of the movie's most unconventional elements. What makes it even more interesting is that the movie also talks about the Mafia code of silence – Omertà (which gives the movie its title). The two, very different sides are contrasted in how they take care of their own and refuse to do anything to harm their organizations. In a way, it tells us, the police force is just as secretive and protected from scrutiny as the mob itself. For any movie that had actual police support and involvement, this is revolutionary. And this movie undoubtedly did have some kind of help from local cops: The late Dennis Farina plays Cusack's partner, Dorato, would go on to a long, illustrious career in TV (*Crime Story* and *Law and Order*) and film (*Get Shorty* and *Out of Sight*). But while this movie was being made, Farina was still a Chicago police officer, moonlighting as an actor. I personally theorize that co-starring in a movie that didn't show police in the most flattering light may have been one factor that led to him becoming a full-time actor not long after this movie was released.

The urban landscapes (Davis's hometown of Chicago, featured in many of his movies from this era) and blood-crazed criminals – the worst played by overacting legend Henry Silva! – make this one a standout among Norris's oeuvres (by the way, Silva would go on to bedevil Seagal as another vicious baddie in the aforementioned *Above the Law*).

One final thought on the movie: There's no love story. I mean, there *kind of* is – with Cusack consoling Diana when her family is killed. But it feels more like a father-daughter or brother-sister bond of sympathy than a sexual or romantic relationship. Cusack truly seems to merely be feeling for the girl's loss – having experienced his own when his father was killed in the line of duty years earlier. While her mob family connections make it a very different kind of duty, Cusack still understands that commitment to both personal and professional families (not to mention that Diana is mentioned as being in her late teens, making her a bit young for the likes of the seasoned Norris).

The big city scenery, complex drama, and corruption subplot all combine to make *Code of Silence* one of the better movies that Norris had made up to this point (or since then, to be perfectly honest). Eddie Cusack isn't so much the traditional tough guy that Norris had grown accustomed to playing. Starring in this rather than another standard karate movie with little-to-no depth meant that Cusack was one of Norris's more nuanced roles. Don't get me wrong! There's still plenty of tough guy shenanigans, macho behavior, and karate kicks. But mostly, that seems just in line with traditional cop behavior than your usual action movie tropes. Cusack's refusal to compromise or give in to corruption, and his status as a second-generation police officer make him far more interesting than Norris's usual "tough guy with a heart" schtick.

Like I said, Davis made a handful of classics in his time behind the camera, which is more than a lot of directors can claim. Among those, *Code of Silence* deserves to still be talked about.

–Kurt Belcher

Invasion U.S.A. (1985)

Hollywood loves an easy villain. Sometimes it's an alien, or a robot, or a clan of ninjas. Sometimes it's a clan of alien robot ninjas. All of them serve the same purpose: being generic, unambiguous bad guys that an audience can watch get murdered in huge numbers without ever feeling guilty about it.

Since 9/11, Middle Eastern terrorists have largely become the U.S. propaganda machine's go-to bogeymen. But in the four decades that bridged the rise of McCarthyism in 1950 and the fall of the Iron Curtain in 1990, no one filled that role better than the Soviet Union and her allies.

While Red Scaremongering on the silver screen never surpassed the heights—and depths—it reached in the '50 and '60s with such films as *The Manchurian Candidate* and *The Green Berets*, the waning days of the Cold War were still a fruitful time for macho-posturing manly men, right-wing super-patriots, and unimaginative screenwriters alike. As with everything else, anti-Communist hysteria only got bigger, louder, and dumber in the 1980s.

To wit, if you think Patrick Swayze battling Bolsheviks in *Red Dawn* was the most absurd, over-the-top example of pinko panic that the Decade of Decadence had to offer, you've clearly never seen 1985's *Invasion U.S.A.*

What could be a greater threat to the all-American, bald eagle, stars-and-stripes way of life than militant Marxists parachuting into a cozy Colorado community? How about a fleet of LCVP boats disgorging a literal *army* of kill-crazy comrades onto the beaches of Florida, where they are then shuttled all across the country via Mack trucks for the sole purpose of causing mass murder and mayhem on a national scale?

And it's set during Christmastime, no less. Take that, capitalist swine!

What's worse, the invaders aren't just targeting military bases and government buildings, but also churches and county fairs, sleepy suburban housing tracts and malls full of last-minute holiday shoppers. Disguised as police officers, they slaughter parties packed with innocent civilians, sparking waves of anti-authority riots. As martial law is declared by our hopelessly inept Big Government, only one rugged individualist boasts enough bearded badassery to restore order: Chuck Norris.

Just like Arnold Schwarzenegger in *Commando*, however, Norris' retired super-soldier isn't interested. While that wimp Arnie spent his downtime feeding deer and sharing ice cream with a pint-sized Alyssa Milano, though, Norris finds fulfillment wrestling alligators and barbecuing frogs. He isn't about to give up such a life of luxury just to help some Deep State stooges cover their asses.

At least, not until his underdeveloped Native American BFF gets caught in the Commies' crossfire.

Before you can say "this time it's personal," Norris is clad head-to-toe in denim, karate-kicking and machine-gunning a bloody swath through legions of faceless henchmen in order to hunt down the sinister Soviets' scheming strategist, played by cult character actor Richard Lynch of *The Sword & the Sorcerer*, *Puppet Master III*, and *Savage Vengeance* "fame."

Director Joseph Zito previously cut his teeth working in the horror genre, helming such memorable splatter fare as *The Prowler* and *Friday the 13th: The Final Chapter*. Fitting, then, that *Invasion U.S.A.* depicts Norris less as a traditional action hero and more like a killer from a slasher film. He stalks his enemies from the shadows, turning predatory pinkos into paranoid prey. Often he simply appears out of nowhere, killing off one or two baddies before vanishing once more into thin air, leaving his remaining victims trembling with the knowledge that *they're next*.

We know virtually nothing about the character's background and personality. Norris barely even talks, to the point where *Invasion U.S.A.* could almost pass as a silent film if not for the nonstop gunfire and explosions. In fact, Norris is such a figure of mystery and terror that the lead villain actually has nightmares about him!

That's not the only way *Invasion U.S.A.* borrows from the horror genre, though. From Dario Argento and Lucio Fulci, it adopts an almost surrealist rejection of conventional narrative structure. Playing like a feverish mosaic of loosely connected carnage set-pieces, *Invasion U.S.A.* isn't quite plotless, but it's damn close.

Meanwhile, from Roger Corman the picture adopts a utilitarian bluntness that removes any and all extraneous details in order to maintain momentum as it rockets towards its climax. There are still faint hints of discarded subplots throughout—most notably the recurring journalist character, presumably once intended as Norris' love interest—but any conflict that cannot be settled with an Uzi is wisely swept aside. In the end, just like one of Corman's creature features, the credits roll as soon as the monster is defeated. No muss, no fuss.

Indeed, despite its faults *Invasion U.S.A.* is never boring. For a Cannon Films production, it actually feels much bigger than its modest $12 million budget would suggest. Lady Luck gifted the director two incredible shooting locations scheduled for demolition—an abandoned residential neighborhood and a shopping mall—and Zito made the most of them, stuffing both to the brim with props and extras. Then he handed Lynch a missile launcher and Norris a pick-up truck and let them go to work.

Even more impressive is the film's final act, which suddenly turns *Invasion U.S.A.* into a full-fledged war picture, only instead of taking place in some bombed-out desert wasteland, the climactic battle—which reportedly cost about half the movie's budget—is set in downtown Atlanta. Army tanks thunder through city streets while helicopters weave between glistening skyscrapers. Hordes of slavering Soviet guerillas clash with battalions of stalwart G.I. Joes.

Surprisingly, though, it all comes down to a respectful debate between political ideologies when the hypocrisies of Lynch's Communist beliefs are tellingly exposed through an insightful, passionate speech which Norris delivers in defense of capitalism and ha ha ha, no he doesn't, Norris just shoots Lynch with a bazooka. That Commie goes boom real good!

A gritty, urban counterpart to the sweaty jungle warfare of *Missing in Action, Invasion U.S.A.* is one of the shiniest, schlockiest jewels in Norris' filmography. Its Reagan-era Republican alarmism and one-man-army power-fantasy excess are only matched by *Death Wish 3*, not coincidentally also a Cannon Films production. Together, these two movies offer a chilling glimpse into the collective id of American conservatism.

But damned if they aren't fun to watch all the same.

–William Tea

The Delta Force (1986)

The Delta Force is one of the many reasons why Chuck Norris has become such a staple in the Hollywood action movie scene. Set in the mid-80s, this movie is full of guns, missiles, and explosions while still delivering the good old fashioned American propaganda that children, teenagers, and adults in the 80s grew up to expect. While many people acknowledge that Chuck Norris facts are full of hyperbole, *The Delta Force* convinced viewers that Chuck Norris could do anything.

Before the movie even begins, an iconic logo that action movie fans have come to know and love pops up on the screen. That's right, Cannon Films! Cannon is no stranger to controversy and this film is no different. Borrowing elements from real life, those associated with the picture wanted Americans to understand that terrorism was a threat at the doorstep of Lady Liberty's house. Luckily, Chuck and Lee Marvin were behind the door, ready to defend her and spread the eagle's wings of justice to protect her children.

I'll admit, as a kid, these types of movies were up my alley. The American hero beating up bad guys trying to hurt freedom loving citizens. Believing the moral of the story to be that justice prevails and liberty sails on to see another day. When one hears the words, Cannon Film, "political" usually isn't the first thought that comes to mind. But I found that as an adult, it was all I could think about with this movie.

What begat what? Were the Americans really the good guys? What had pushed these men to want to hijack a plane? What was the point of all of it? Don't get me wrong – those that want to harm the innocent are not heroes and their cause is not just. But what drives a human being to reach a point where they believe their cause is greater than human life?

My brain was filled with questions as I watched on. There was more to this movie than I remembered. It was confirmed when a Holocaust tattoo flashed across the screen. Since many of us have been alive, we have felt the tension between countries in the Middle East. This movie takes a hold of that and slaps us in the face with it. You wanted to turn your brain off and watch an action flick? Nope, not here. While we look to media as an aid to save our sanity from all of the horrors in the world, *The Delta Force* tells us that conflict is alive and well, even in 2020.

I wasn't expecting to face such emotion in this film. I was hoping to chant, "USA!" after everything was said and done. Yet, there I sat, teary eyed as Hanna Schygulla cried out as Ingrid that she would not separate the Jewish passports from the rest after the hijackers asked her to do so. And when Martin Balsam stood up after hearing his character's name called, his wife begging and pleading him not to leave, and he looks at her and says, "We survived once. We can do it again." A child screams and cries for her father as he's led away. A priest willing to submit himself as a hostage as he states that he is Jewish because Christ was Jewish. These scenes were in this movie?! Did I watch the wrong film? I wasn't supposed to feel like this, dammit!

I would be lying if I said I wasn't looking for some ass kicking to happen. After that tough scene on the plane, I needed to see these guys pay for what they did. Needless to say, when Chuck Norris found out all of this was happening and was on his way to save the passengers, I was relieved. Now we're getting into the movie I expected and remembered – over the top and full of one-liners.

While the movie does try to take itself seriously, there are plenty of reminders that this is an action film and not a drama waiting for its Emmy nomination. Chuck Norris and his missile launching dirt bike? Please and thank you! Menahem Golan and James Bruner knew what they were doing when writing this film. It's not every day that an action film borrows from real life events and plays on the emotions of people that have witnessed such experiences. That's what they were aiming to do, and I think they succeeded. But there was just enough cheese to bring me back down and to enjoy it for what it was – an action film starring Chuck Norris.

Another thing this movie does well is show us that not every story has a happy ending. Sure, Chuck saves the day but at what cost? Lives were still lost on the side of the good guys. With every great story, comes some sort of sacrifice. Chuck loses his friend at the end. It's a somber reminder of knowing what they signed up for when joining the Army. It's the ultimate sacrifice. *The Delta Force* wants people to recognize that a price comes with freedom.

One of the joys I get out of life is to revisit media to see how my views and thoughts have changed. Movies are one of my favorite mediums to review. As a kid, it was the good guys versus the bad guys, and gosh darn it, the good guys saved the day again. As an adult, it's not so black and white. Did the Cannon Group actually accomplish what it was setting out to do? Was I supposed to question these things after watching this film? Am I looking into this way too much? Ask me again when I revisit the film in ten years.

–John Bruske

Firewalker (1986)

All my other chapters in this book are of early Chuck Norris movies, dating back to when him figuring out his screen persona or even before that. This one is heyday Chuck, released right after *The Delta Force* in 1986, at a point where he clearly felt that he was ready to attempt something new. *Firewalker* was definitely a new approach for him, being a comedy, a buddy movie and an Indiana Jones ripoff all in one, and, while the movie is absolutely as bad as people make out, it's not bad because Chuck Norris was trying something new. I rather like his comedy. I wish he'd do more of it. Someone team him up with Jackie Chan!

He's Max Donigan and he's half of a treasure hunting partnership with Leo Porter, played by Louis Gossett Jr. This double act works far better than it should and isn't only Leo getting them into trouble and Max roundhouse kicking their way back out of it. That said, there's a bar fight in Mexico that's absolutely priceless. Gossett does try. Against a huge Mexican, Miguel Ángel Fuentes. He also fails inevitably while Norris sits back and chews gum. Then Chuck steps up to show him how it's done. It's a fantastic scene and, if the whole movie was as good as that one scene, you'd know it as well as you know *Die Hard*, *The Terminator* and *Raiders of the Lost Ark*. Of course, it isn't. Which is why you don't.

Max and Leo start the film in a jeep being chased through a desert by well armed people in dune buggies. They're staked out on the sand by a Chinese general with a scar on his face and a lackey to hold his parasol. He tells them it would be inhuman to leave them there without water, so he puts a Perrier into Chuck's hand. Which is tied to a stake. But our tough hero crushes the Perrier bottle, cuts himself free and next thing we know, this intrepid duo are in a bar fitting the bill of the "men of, shall we say, questionable character" that Patricia Goodwin's searching for. She's Melody Anderson, best known for playing Dale Arden in *Flash Gordon*.

Somewhere here, the plot manifests itself but how was never quite clear to me. Patricia has had visions all her life and she has a treasure map and it'll lead to a lot of gold. They just need to avoid the red cyclops with the long black hair and figure out what the map is supposed to depict and then they'll be on their way to collect this hoard of Aztec, Mayan, Spanish, Apache, Egyptian gold. Or something like that. It doesn't matter. What matters is that they get there, very possibly by letting a sleepy Patricia thrust a magical jewelled dagger into a map of Central America without looking. No, I'm not kidding. There's lazy writing and then there's this.

Anyway, they set off into what I presume is supposed to be Honduras disguised as two priests and a nun — "Just act wise and holy," suggests Chuck—and, amazingly given how this sentence began, it promptly gets really boring. It does perk up when our heroes are saved from certain decapitation at the hands of armed guerrillas by John Rhys Davies, who's some sort of batshit crazy mercenary generalissimo called Corky Taylor with dreams of becoming a king. His scenes are glorious but completely unnecessary, except to wake us up again after ten minutes in the jungle that I think I slept through.

What follows is exactly what you'd expect from a film that rips off everything it can think of with abandon. There's *Raiders of the Lost Ark* in here, *Romancing the Stone*, *Crocodile Dundee*, you name it. What that means is that there's nothing here that's close to either original or coherent, but it checks off all the bingo bits. There's swinging. There's rock climbing. There's sliding under stone doors just before they close forever. Of course, there's saving the damsel in distress. And of course, there's find the temple, even though there's absolutely no pretence given to how they do so. At the requisite moment in the film, they simply look up and there it is.

There's Sonny Landham from *Predator* looking evil in an eyepatch, Louis Gossett Jr. hanging by his wrists above a misting pool and Chuck Norris doing cool things with knives. There's a running joke here that he can't hit anything with a gun but he's an old pro with throwing knives. I quite like the running jokes, many of which fall on Chuck. He's astoundingly naïve, paying $12 for three drinks in a two-bit town in Mexico. He sleeps through all the good bits, like the flight to San Miguel; they land with one engine on fire and the passengers all in a panic and he wakes up fresh as a daisy, saying, "Great flight, huh?"

Norris also gets the best lines, whether they're meant to be funny or serious. That big Mexican insults him in Spanish, which Max doesn't speak, so Leo translates. "He said your mother was a pig and your father was a dog." Unconcerned Chuck deadpans, "He mention my sister?" A more serious moment compares Leo being scared of not having his friend, who may have been eaten by an alligator, with Max, who's scared of suits, alarm clocks and apartment buildings. I like that.

This may be the most ridiculous Chuck Norris movie ever made and I say that having already reviewed *Slaughter in San Francisco*, but all its faults lie in the script, which should never ever ever have been greenlit. They don't lie in Chuck Norris trying comedy for a change and sending up his tough guy persona in the process. That's rather a lot of fun.

Oh, and I must visit the restaurant at the end. It's Le Kliff, in Puerto Vallarta, Mexico. Go away, COVID. I need to eat.

–Hal CF Astell

Chuck Norris and the Karate Kommandos (1986)

In the 1980s a good sign that you were making it as a multimedia starlet was that someone gave you a cartoon. Imagine being a living breathing person and having the honor of fighting evil shoulder to shoulder with the likes of Optimus Prime, He-Man and Rainbow Brite. To be a real person and be so mythical that the only way your legend can be told is through the medium of 1980s cartoons was indeed a rare honor. Few men have this honor: Mr. T, Hulk Hogan, and of course, Chuck Norris.

Chuck Norris and the Karate Kommandos premiered in 1986 from Ruby-Spears, a group of defectors from Hanah Barbara, who gave us properties like *Pac-Man, Turbo Teen*, and *Centurions*. It lasted a scant five episodes but packs a lot of action into those few. As the name implies, Church Norris is the hero, but he's joined by an elite team of "Kommandos" that I like to imagine he recruited personally.

Norris's elite team of Kommandos includes Kimo who is described as "A Samurai Warrior," which is kind of his entire character. Kimo is stoic, tough, and ready to draw swords and chop what needs chopping. There's Tabe, a Sumo champion who despite being the comedy relief is quite competent in combat, it does my heart good to see us fatties represented on the team. In real life Sumo wrestlers are fat, but also abnormally strong and fast and Tabe seems to share these traits, overpowering the bad guys with sheer power. Next up are Pepper and Reed, a brother and sister team with Reed being Norris' young protege and Pepper being a technical genius. Reed functions as Norris' sidekick and confidant while his sister Pepper helps with technical assets. Finally, we have the viewer analog, a sassy young troublemaker nicknamed Too Much. Unlike most tag-along kids in cartoons, Too Much is far more than a part-time hostage. Sure, he gets captured a lot, but that kid doesn't take it lying down. He kicks, bites and sasses the bad guys and even helps out in battle. Too Much is actually, dare I say…likeable! The show gives every member of the Karate Kommandos a chance to shine.

One can't have good heroes without despicable villains, and this show's villains are… meh. Our bad guys are mostly generic ninjas, led by the generically named "Super Ninja," who seems to have serious beef with Chuck Norris. Every time Norris is even *mentioned* Super Ninja flies into a seething rage, and this remarkable hatred for Chuck Norris is never once explained. I mean, I get that he's the villain and Chuck is the good guy, but this isn't just a "He foiled my plans again" kinda hatred. It's as if Chuck Norris did some horrible, unforgivable wrong to Super Ninja just before the series started. Rounding out the bad guys is the Mastermind behind it all known simply as The Klaw. He calls the shots, makes the plans, and ups the dough for the insidious plans of the bad guys. Like most cartoon villains, he escapes at the last minute but lacks the charisma of the 80s criminal masterminds. There are a few other villains that pop up through the show's short run, like Angelfish and Mask. These folks don't show up multiple times, but I like to think if the show ran for more than five episodes, we would have seen more of them. I didn't delve into the expanded material of the show like the comics from Marvel's Star imprint and storybooks, maybe there's more to the mythology. Even at five episodes, though, they did manage to crank out a toy line.

It's interesting that, in this show, Chuck Norris speaks for himself and the character in the show is pretty much just real-life Chuck. The hero here isn't super, he doesn't fly or shoot lasers out of his eyes… he just does martial arts really, really well. He faces bad guys with courage, leads his people effectively, and is ethical. You can totally believe that, if shit went down in real life, the living and breathing Chuck Norris would be about the same. Slinging commands, making ultimatums and, if need be, kicking ass. I point to an incident in Austin, Texas where three men tried to mug Chuck Norris and wound up with what the police described as, "seriously broken arms.". Dude has five black belts and is a veteran. If faced with a bunch of evil ninjas I think he could totally handle himself.

Chuck himself does the live-action intros and outros of every show where he details the morals of the episodes, everything from "Bullying is bad" to "We all make mistakes." It is pretty clever how he's always on a Total Gym for these spots but you gotta rep your brand, right? Chuck seems a little unprepared for the wackiness of 80s cartoons, especially taking lines like "laser robot" and "island of the dead" seriously so it feels like these host sequences were tacked on later to pad the episodes out. That could be a reasonable take, since other than a brief mention of the episode's plot the "morals" seem to have little to do with the narratives themselves.

Since I was born in 1980, I have a soft spot for goofy 80s cartoons. I enjoy the black and white morals as well as the sharp and undeniable line between good and evil. The good guys are strong, noble, brave, and kind while the bad guys are cruel, selfish, and ultimately cowardly. There is no ambiguity in these shows, good is good, bad is bad and the only thing the two can do is fight and, as always, the good guys win. Sure, it's goofy, and some parts of it didn't age too well. The animation has flaws, and the story lacks depth, but when you are home from school and sitting in front of a tube TV in the living room in 1986, this was the height of entertainment.

–Joshua Knode

Braddock: Missing in Action III (1988)

Propaganda movies come in all shapes and sizes. I'm fascinated by them because of how they run the gamut of the utterly laughable, like John Wayne's *The Green Berets,* to others that are so subtle in their promotion of empire or of the military-industrial complex, that you wouldn't have ever guessed you were watching any kind of propaganda.

Chuck Norris movies, of course, are firmly in the laughable category. But most of us put up with this ageless movie star's obsessive political posturing because, well, we like cheesy movies. Most critically minded movie goers simply roll their eyes at Chuck's latest absurd political rants, and happily indulge once in a while in his prolific contributions to the nostalgic world of '80's action movies.

These shoot 'em up, kick their ass films are getting a little bit harder to swallow, though, as more Vietnam-like forever wars continue to exhaust a war-weary United States. So, the undoubtedly 'roided up action stars you'd see in '80's high octane 'Merica movies like Chuck's *Braddock: Missing in Action III* parading around shirtless in hostile territory seemingly impervious to gunfire coming from all directions, while effortlessly mowing down whole battalions at a time...well, it's a tad less fun watching them these days. Decades of endless wars that have bankrupted the country and sent thousands of veterans' home in body bags or to wither away on our streets have sobered up the whole experience of watching these kind of films. At least for me, anyway.

Braddock MIA III, though, started off very well with terrific production value of a falling Saigon, and immediately delved into the heartbreaking separation of Chuck's character, Col. James Braddock, and his Vietnamese wife in a dizzying case of mistaken identity, in which he thinks she has been killed amidst the chaos of that day.

If you stopped at that point of the film and thought too much about this, though, you'd suddenly find yourself mired in more continuity problems than the dense jungle that Chuck found himself in once he returned to the badlands of Vietnam! Wife? I remember someone mentioning that he had a wife back in the States in the second *Missing in Action*!

Sorry to digress. Back to the story. After many years of a brooding and lonesome existence, Chuck bumps into a priest stateside at a bar who informs him that his wife and child are still alive back in Vietnam. Initially he doesn't believe it, but soon makes his way back to 'Nam to save his family from an evil general who's been holding them captive.

When Chuck finally catches up to his Vietnamese wife, a lovely Miki Kim, their love story is very earnest and genuine. There's great chemistry between the two, and Chuck Norris' emotionally driven performance is very impressive. I give Chuck some serious acting props up to this point in the movie. I was starting to wonder how I was going to write an essay poking fun at him.

Well, that worry disappeared real quick as he quipped, "I don't step on toes, I step on necks," to a U.S. official warning him not to go save anyone back in 'Nam. I knew that was the beginning of the end of the serious filmmaking. Oh well, the drama was surprisingly decent while it lasted.

Before you knew it, Chuck was running around the jungle bare-chested in what looked like pajama bottoms. Not only did he avoid getting shot by dozens of soldiers firing seemingly thousands of rounds at him, but how he didn't get cut up in that jungle dressed like that I'll never know. And his poor long lost Vietnamese wife met a very unromantic end with a bullet to the head by the sadistic general, which also killed any more love stories of any kind for the rest of the movie. You could tell Chuck and his producers all had quite a bit enough of the sappy stuff. It was time to go blow shit up.

Not to jump too far ahead, but Chuck winds up kicking this general's ass along with his entire army so efficiently with barely a scratch (even after being tortured), that I wondered why he didn't just make his way up to Hanoi and take over the entire damn country himself.

Once the action really gets going, Chuck's ego got the best of him as his role steadily declined into individual superhero fantasy feats of utter absurdity. I mean, Chuck wasn't even hiding behind anything when he was returning fire with the general's soldiers...who happen to be the worst shots in the history of any army. They couldn't hit the broad side of a barn! Chuck just remained unflappable in the middle of the road, minus the shirt, not even trying to get out of the way of the multitudes of bullets coming his way, just picking off the hapless soldiers one by one with his...gun? That thing was more a hybrid of everything from a Swiss Army Knife (yes, a knife jutted out of it) to a surface to air missile to a rocket propelled grenade launcher to a flame thrower to a machine gun. Tony Montana, eat your heart out.

I know, it's an '80s action movie. It's supposed to be crazy and over-the-top. I get it. And I give the movie a lot of credit for trying at times to be serious, not only about the love story but concerning itself with the plight of Amerasian children who languished in Vietnam after the war.

But the xenophobic stench started to get a little rancid after a while. And it made me wonder if saving all the children held captive by the devilish general was just a cynical way of using them as a human shield type subplot, serving to deflect from an otherwise gross overdose of Chuck Norris flavored right-wing propaganda.

But, hey, it was way better than John Wayne's *Green Berets*.

–Jed Rowen

Hero and the Terror (1988)

Here is an anomaly in the canon of Chuck Norris. *Hero and the Terror* is surprising for its effectively sensitive portrayal of a romantic relationship. Norris delivers one of his most focused and committed performances. Some suspense and atmosphere are even developed along the way. Where it falls short, however, is in the presence of the titular Terror. He is a one-dimensional killing machine, of the Jason Voorhees or Michael Myers variety, *sans* mask. That choice feels lazy, like an opportunity squandered.

All in all, though, this uneven stew adds up to an okay B action movie. It stands out – a little - from the typical Cannon fodder of the 1980s. That is to say, there are worse ways to waste an hour and a half.

The movie opens as Danny O'Brien (Chuck Norris), an undercover cop, is stalking a serial killer - known as the Terror - on a deserted pier. It is cluttered with little commercial shacks and restaurants. Danny ventures inside one called Sinbad's and finds the requisite killer's lair, complete with a dead body storage room. He is attacked by the killer – a brute named Simon Moon (Jack O'Halloran) – and is nearly killed. In the end, he subdues the brute just as back-up arrives.

It is a suspenseful and admirably restrained scene. The photography (by Eric Van Haren Noman) is atmospheric.

It turns out to be a nightmare - O'Brien's memories of a killer he took down a year before these events. It is the incident that earned him the public moniker of Hero. But Danny wears the title reluctantly, and still quakes in fear at memories of how close he came to losing it all that day.

Now Danny is helping Kay (Brynn Thayer), his pregnant fiancée, move into his place. She was his therapist, it turns out, who helped him through his trauma after his *duel a' mort* with the Terror. Talk about conflict of interest! - Still, the relationship is handled with much more detail and sensitivity than one expects from a Chuck Norris vehicle. A surprising amount of time is spent on these scenes, which do not really propel the plot, but which enrich its characters.

The actors are up to it, too. Norris has rarely, if ever, been so committed to his character's humanity, beyond the fights on the mean streets. There is a clarity in his work here that reveals lots of personal work as an actor. But even better is Brynn Thayer as Kay. She has been a reliable dramatic character actor in television for several decades. Her professionalism and experience shine here. She is terrific and complex. Lesser actors often shine when working with masters of the craft, and I think some of that may be at work here in Norris's favor.

While all the lovey-dovey stuff is going on, however, the Terror is thinking about hatey-hate. He breaks out of prison (using an unlikely combination of lip balm, tooth-floss and iron filings to saw through bars), steals a van, and crashes the main gate. However, he loses control of the vehicle and steers it off of a sheer cliff into the Snake River. It is a spectacular car crash, well-shot on a budget.

Everyone assumes that the Terror is now dead, even though no body is recovered. Guess what? He isn't. He manages to make a new lair in the run-down and boarded-up Wiltern Theater in Los Angeles. He is up to his old tricks again, and the bodies begin to pile up in a hidden prop room.

Danny, still being a Chuck Norris character, feels his spider senses tingling even before there is any real evidence. He is convinced the Terror is back, and inhabiting the run-down theater, even though nobody believes him.

Much time is wasted searching the theater to no avail. These scenes are interesting still, because of their effective use of the backstage areas of an old vaudeville era theater. If you have every had the opportunity to explore one of these grand old theaters, you will know how unique and creepy they can be. This movie showcases that side of LA's magnificent Wiltern theater to great advantaged.

Then the Wiltern is refurbished and re-opened with a theatrical event, which the mayor is slated to attend. The city comes to the Terror, and he has a supply of fresh meat - starting with the actress who stars in the stage show.

There is plenty of kick-butt action, as is requisite for a Chuck Norris film, and most of it is routine, but badly needed in order to ramp up the pace, which has repeatedly screeched to a halt for the scenes between Danny and Kay.

There are also the typical clichés. Danny's partner Robinson (Steve James), for instance, *must* die at the hands of the Terror. And he does, making it personal for Danny, even though it already was. The scene is interesting. The murder is inter-cut with Danny and Kay in the maternity ward, as she gives birth. Robinson dies as another soul is born.

It's too bad there aren't more provocative moments like that in *Hero and the Terror*. Danny predictably fights and defeats the Terror once and for all, saving his new family in the process.

Jack O'Halloran is generally a pretty effective heavy. Sometimes more than that, as in Dick Richard's *Farewell My Lovely*, playing the love-sick thug, Moose Malloy. It is a shame he is not given more to do here. He gnashes his teeth and looks scary, but we don't know why he does what he does. Even his therapist (Billy Drago) says he just kills because he likes killing. Period.

I just wanted to like it more.

This movie wants to be two things. A sensitively drama about a romantic relationship, and a fast-paced action-thriller about a duel between a cop and a lawless brute. The two sides are at odds with one another, and therein lies the fatal flaw of *Hero and the Terror*.

–Ron Ford

Delta Force 2: The Columbian Connection (1990)

SUPER: RIO DE JANEIRO. CANNON STYLE.

Mardi Gras is in full swing and Ramon Cota (Billy Drago, *The Untouchables*) knows the password for the house holding a giant masquerade. Dressed in his chintzy *Eyes Wide Shut* gear as he sets up agents trying to capture him. Drago leads them successfully to their doom and gets to tell an agent (the legend Richard Jaeckel, *King of the Kickboxers*) that no one can arrest him, so it is fruitless to try.

CUT TO:

Chuck Norris, Cannon-era Chuck Norris returns as Colonel Scott McCoy, just chillin' with a Delta Force buddy and his peeps at a restaurant before he has to get up and settle a disruptive customer. In classic Norris fashion before finishing dinner, of course. Meanwhile, Billy Drago heads back to his ranch. He's lost eight shipments of cocaine to the DEA, so he's understandably pissed. To show how pissed he kills a worker woman's husband and takes away her baby until she lets Drago release his own little dragon… and then he kills the baby. I know…a guy we all want to work for, right?

Chuck goes in for a briefing with the General Taylor (John P. Ryan, *The Right Stuff*) and Jaeckel on Cota, following which they meet with a Cota defector intent on selling his employer down the river because of the aforementioned incident with murder, rape and dead babies. Chuck is excited about flying first class, so they catch a plane and go and slap the cuffs on Billy Drago before throwing him out of a perfectly good aeroplane.

"Oh, shit!"

Chuck flies like an eagle baby, saving Drago before he plummets to his death as the General lovingly wills Chuck to victory like Bette Midler from a distance. Drago is put on trial, but the bail is pocket change to a well-seasoned drug lord like him. Still, he's not the kind of man that holds a grudge, although he walks out of court secretly planning to even the score with Norris, which he manages to do while Chuck goes to film a basketball game. After the game Drago kills Chuck's buddy's wife and son.

GAME ON, DELTA FORCE!

Chuck's buddy vows revenge and even dusts the back of Chuck's head with a pistol so he cannot interfere with his plan of whacking Drago with a polo mallet. Richard Jaeckel shows up and tells Chuck's buddy killing Drago is cool, but they have to do it right. This becomes a foolish pause in Jaeckel's plan which sees both he and his crew become Cota's prisoners.

Drago takes his prisoners back to his compound, there exposing the traitor in his midst, dispatching him using the same tricky-knife-flicky finishing move he used on a field worker earlier in the movie. All while attempting to gas Chuck Norris. Big mistake!

The General gives a rousing smackdown to the stateside press regarding the involvement of Delta Force as the El Presidente of Drago's cocaine paradise bitches that the world thinks they are all a bunch of pushers.

CUT TO:

Chuck gets to see his buddy's death on video before the customary "Norris preps for battle" montage. With his fun-loving bunch of bullshit commandoes, Chuck heads in for a briefing about the best way to take down Cota's impregnable fortress until the General is called away to answer the red phone.

"That was the President," says the General (Ryan at his bombastic best). There is a window open for the Delta Force to fly in and start some shit and they will need to be ready. So, they do a little more training…in a montage.

Then: All three DEA agents will be executed because of an embargo forced on the cocaine kingdom by the U. S. commander and chief. The ticking clock is on. The Delta Force are going in. Chuck has to climb a ridiculously steep rock wall before hooking up with an asset in-country, who just so happens to be the woman Cota raped after killing her husband but before killing her child. See where this is going?

Wildcard (Chuck's call sign) calls, "Stranglehold is a go!" so the big compound battle cut together with Chuck finally getting Drago is how the film slowly draws to an end in a sadly predictable, Lee Marvin-free finale: a lot of big explosions, people dying while flying through the air, Drago seductively monologuing, the final confrontation clumsy and far from satisfying.

What we want by this point is Drago versus Norris which, unlike the build-up, is over quickly, and, unlike the first *Delta Force*, Chuck doesn't get to sign off doing something cool (like killing Robert Forster with tiny rockets mounted to the rear of his dirt bike). No folks, second time 'round all Chuck chiefly gets to do is watch one of Drago's droogs setup his eventual demise by slicing the rope holding them to the evacuating chopper.

Chuck's job is to, quite literally, wait for the rope to break, watch Billy Drago fall straight to Hell, and see the credits begin quickly because this is Cannon movie and the budget has just run out… and that's all she wrote. End scene.

–Kent Hill

The Hitman (1991)

When you are one of the greatest action stars to ever hit the silver screen, even some of your mediocre efforts can wow your super fans. If you're smart though, like Sly Stallone, Arnold and the subject of our book here, Chuck Norris, trying something outside of your comfort zone like TV with the popular series, *Walker, Texas Ranger* can be just lightning in a bottle you need as an aging star. During the early 90s, that transition was wise choice, but before raking in the mega bucks at CBS, Norris starred in the ultra-violent gangster film, *The Hitman.* Chuck teams up with some of the usual suspects for this 1991 production -- his brother, Aaron Norris, and the fine folks at Cannon Pictures.

The Hitman begins like many a buddy cop film with our two detectives, Cliff Garrett (Chuck Norris) and Ronny Delaney (Michael Parks, *Red State, From Dusk Till Dawn*) on a stakeout. Both appear to have some wonderful comradery. Ronny is crass and grumpy and possibly has some of the best lines in the film. When Ronny mumbles "I'm so horny, I could fuck mud!" this writer giggled like a twelve year-old. Both men are looking to nab some drug dealers waiting for a massive shipment. Garrett's looking to go and arrest the goons while they're in the midst of cracking crates open filled with narcotics. Ronny isn't quite as frisky and thinks it nothing. The men become separated and it's all up to Garrett to get things done. After plowing through some baddies, Cliff gets confronted by Ronny who, to his shock is a dirty cop. Ronny proceeds to pump some rounds into his partner, who then falls out a two-story building onto the concrete and left for dead

Amazingly, Garrett survives the vicious attack from Ronny and is now clinging to life in a coma. After some serious TLC and rehab, Garrett comes back as an undercover hitman for the mob. He also has a new name – Grogan. Grogan is now working for Italian mafioso, Marco Luganni (Al

Waxman, *Atlantic City, Cagney & Lacey*). The name change isn't the only difference we are treated to in this transformation for a hero. We are also treated to a glorious, flowing mullet that now hangs from the back of Chuck's head. To me, once I saw the mullet, I knew it was going to be hell for anyone who crosses his path.

As Luganni's right hand man, Grogan unleashes his will on rival mobsters with his trusty shotgun and hands of stone. Chuck doesn't quite rely on the martial arts combat he's known for here, but he does show some welcome flashes during a couple ass beatings. Luganni thinks Grogan is his right hand man but little does he know, Grogan's looking to bring him down, as well as the other various mob scum around town.

Next to *Invasion USA, The Hitman* is easily the most violent and action-packed Chuck Norris feature. While not as mean spirited as *Invasion* was, I was kind of floored by the super racist dialogue that came out the character's mouths. Some of the shit Ronny's says is pretty cringe-worthy. That said, it turns him into a great villain. Michael Parks is such an unheralded talent. Tarantino and Kevin Smith got Parks rolling with some more fine performances and well deserved critical acclaim later in his career. Parks does have a strong appreciation from his peers and thankfully his more recent ventures have translated to more fanfare. His turn as Ronny Delaney is just another excellent performance that shows off the ability of one of the finer character actors of our time.

In the midst of all the shoot-outs, exploding bodies and ghastly mob torture, Grogan surprisingly finds himself mentoring a bullied neighbor kid. Grogan may be a hard ass, but he's got soft side too. There's a tiny bit of *Karate Kid* during these scenes, but it's not too forced and soon we get back to the REAL action when Ronny comes back on the scene to surprise Grogan. After about an hour with his character off screen, adding a maniacal killer like Ronny back to the fold takes *The Hitman* to another level.

As mentioned earlier, Chuck's bro, Aaron Norris is on hand for the directorial duties. I'm sure Chuck Norris had a big part on the direction of the feature but Aaron is certainly no slouch, especially when it comes to action films. The younger Norris is still working currently with stunt gigs on recent blockbusters like Marvel's *Ant Man.* If you see the name Harry Alan Towers in the credits -- that is not a typo. Yes, that is the legendary British cult film producer extraordinaire. I was surprised myself but if you go through his filmography, it's not just genre classics from the likes of Jess Franco (*The Bloody Judge, Venus in Furs*), he's also produced numerous Cannon titles with both Chuck and Aaron. The talent doesn't end there as we also have Emmy award winner Don Carmody (*Chicago, Porky's*) on hand for the writing duties. There is an interesting mix of talent here but that could be why *The Hitman* works.

By 1991, Chuck Norris had put in more than two decades of work in Hollywood. You'd think by the 90s he wouldn't be capable of displaying the magic of some of his early 80s hits, but he does just that here. Michael Parks and Al Waxman certainly help with their amusing performances as the leading gutter slime baddies. *The Hitman* still doesn't work without the man with the mullet. If you like your action films gritty and violent, *The Hitman* is top-notch entertainment.

–Jeff Dolniak

Sidekicks (1992)

Let's face it; no one likes to admit they were wrong. And certainly no one like to admit that fact in print. And most definitely no one likes to admit that when it comes to Chuck Norris. And yet I recently faced that moment after watching 1992's *Sidekicks*. I mean, honestly, it might be less embarrassing to admit to being a chronic masturbator, a Trump supporter or to owning every Nickelback CD, though, only one of those is truly embarrassing (spoiler: It's Nickelback). So, when I set myself the task of watching *Sidekicks*, I came prepared to hate it; to mock it; to take joy in eviscerating it. But I have failed in that endeavor. As much as it pains me to admit it, I... I... liked it. Oh, fuck it, yes it was fun, and I laughed and despite it being entirely predictable (how could it not), I enjoyed it. Not least of the reasons for this cathartic admission has to do with the fact that Norris himself is essentially a supporting actor in his own film. And then add in that the cast featured the truly unparalleled talent of Mako, plus a decent Beau Bridges, and well...it works.

Now don't get me wrong, this ain't no Aaron Sorkin masterpiece of dialogue nor David Fincher directed gem. It achieves exactly what most movies seek to do; be entertaining and make money. On both counts, it succeeded. But then again, most Norris vehicles make money. There will always be asshats with Ford F-950s and truck nuts dangling from the trailer hitch to make sure that is true. So, the fact that it succeeded in being entertaining, and not ironically so, is the true surprise here. From the outset we follow the story of daydreamer Barry, played by Jonathan Brandis, who was actually a 90s heartthrob, which says more about the 90s than anything else. Brandis is fine, and I'm sure a nice guy, but exudes the sex appeal of the dude making your sandwich at Subway on any given Tuesday. Which is not to take away from Subway employees, especially those who work on Tuesdays, but let's face it, if your fantasizing about the guy slapping provolone on your 6-inch and then slathering it with mayo, you may have an issue. Or perhaps just a healthy cheese/sex fetish, but I digress. Barry is a daydreamer, always working in his idol (enter Chuck Norris) at the center of his fantasies of daring do. His father (Beau Bridges) is concerned of course, as is his thoroughly hot teacher, played by Julia Nickson-Soul. Thankfully she also makes regular appearances in Barry's daydreams, because if she didn't, well that would just be weird. Not as weird as fantasizing about slathering your six-inch with provolone and mayo, but weird. Dad and teacher worry about Barry and thus, the path has been paved for the great Mako to be brought in as the reluctant Dojo to teach Barry the skills he needs after the bad Dojo (Joe Piscopo) basically says "I won't teach you karate, kid" (See what I did there?)

I did mention Aaron Sorkin had nothing to do with this, correct? So, of course, we move effortlessly toward THE BIG TOURNAMENT. As if that wasn't going to happen. And of course, who should show up, but CHUCK NORRIS. And not just any Chuck Norris, but pre-*Walker, Texas Ranger* Chuck Norris. In fact, *Sidekicks* was his last movie before the TV series mainstreamed him. While most would say *WTR* was where Norris was introduced to a network audience, there's a good case to be made that *Sidekicks* already did that the year before. It was aimed at a family demographic, one that wasn't necessarily familiar with Norris before that. It's possible that we would never have had *WTR* if *Sidekicks* had been a flop. Which, now that I think about it, means I really should hate it all the more. The fact that I don't is a compliment in itself. Mako's character manages to convince Norris to participate in the tournament, which is totally implausible until we learn that Norris really wants to teach Piscopo's character a lesson, so it totally makes sense, right? Riiight. Anyway, pretty quickly Norris beats the shit out of Piscopo, which is (let's be honest) thoroughly enjoyable and probably went a long way to my overall embrace of this movie, because that has been my longtime fantasy ever since The Whiners on *SNL* (look it up).

I have some odd fantasies, I realize.

It's also worth pointing out that Norris does his ass-kicking in this movie with a light touch, so to speak. No weapons. No broken necks. And always with the intention to teach a lesson, which again, is more in the *WTR* mode than *The Hitman* or *Code of Silence*. Now we've set up our big showdown; a tiebreaker between Piscopo's team and Mako's team and just as one would expect, Barry is paired up against Piscopo's top student, a guy named Cellini, played by John Buchanan, who obviously missed his calling of being an 80s teen B-movie douchebag by being born too late. How can they inspire Barry? Naturally, it is to set his bricks on fire for the big Breaking Contest. And how does Barry do? Do I really need to tell you? He wins the big contest, of course. And just to prove how much of a win it is? Chuck Norris disappears. Was he ever even there? If an ego falls in the woods and no one hears it, does it still get points on the back end of the movie deal? Call your agent. But now I know why I liked this movie so much. Chuck Norris vanished. A truly happy ending. Not as happy as slathering mayo on your six-inch with provolone, but happy.

Definitely NOT weird.

–Jon Arking

Wind in the Wire (1993)

Wind in the Wire is a Chuck Norris movie in the same way that *Tarantula* is a Clint Eastwood vehicle: He's only in one scene, and it takes almost an hour to get there. Not only is it a stretch to call this a Chuck Norris movie, but it is also equally an act of contortion to call it a movie, period, beyond the fact that it was captured on film, edited, and aired on television.

It was written and directed by Jim Shea, whose other credits are mostly country or country rock music videos, and pop star documentaries. Currently he is at work on an untitled documentary about the great Leon Redbone. That one veers from the easy listening bent of most of his other work. It is one I plan to take a look at when it becomes available.

This 1993 excursion, aired on The Nashville Network, was made to coincide with the release of Randy Travis's album of the same name. It is, in fact, a collection of music videos of songs from the album, strung loosely together by a sketch of a plot depicting a singer/actor (Randy, playing himself) who befriends a homeless runaway boy while he is shooting a western movie in New Mexico, and, for some inconceivable reason, Hawaii.

The plot elements, as to be expected, are handled with the worst kind of sentimentalism. The writing never rises even to a Hallmark Channel level, and nothing in it rings true (with the possible exception of one single line, which I will elucidate upon at the end of this review). Nothing is learned about the boy's background except that he ran away from a group home, and that he has an estranged sister someplace in the country. That is probably just as well, however. If they had tried to fill out the boy's background, I feel quite certain that it would have been with tired old TV movie clichés, ringing just as hollowly as the rest of this turgid hodge-podge.

With a running time of an hour and fourteen minutes long, it plays like three and a half hours. It is a slog, unless you love Randy Travis music. Spoiler alert: I do not. And that is not just a knee-jerk, "all country music sucks" kind of remark. I *love* traditional country music more than just about anything. Travis's cross-over crooning won't commit to being either pop music or western music. Instead, it is just some soulless, commercial thing that lies meaninglessly in between the two.

The thing that keeps you going while watching *Wind in the Wire* is the anticipation of seeing the guest stars promised in the opening credits: Burt Reynolds. Lou Diamond Phillips. Dale Robertson. Denver Pyle. The aforementioned Chuck Norris. Other names turn up as well along the way, including the ever-reliable Peter Jason and the ever-mugging Charles Nelson Reilly, to name just a couple. Most of these celebrities play themselves and are supposedly guest stars in the western shoot that is the framing conceit for this time waster. None of them are given too much to do, and Lord knows how they got them all gathered for this extended piece of ego-boo. But clearly some record company was pumping a butte-load of money into the promotion of Randy's new (at the time) album.

Chuck Norris - the reason we are here, folks – first turns up forty-four minutes into the picture. He is discovered riding a horse in a montage scene that illustrates the film crew's arrival in Hawaii; supposedly to finish shooting their "western." In fact, I'll wager Chuck agreed to do this bore-fest only for the free trip to Hawaii. A few minutes later, we see the abrasive director torturing poor Randy by having him do countless takes of a scene where Chuck Norris kicks his ass with a roundhouse boot. Yes. Cowboys fight with martial arts here. But only in one scene. I don't think Chuck has even one scripted line.

I kept waiting for Charles Nelson Reilly to show up, thinking I may have missed him in the shuffle. But no, he' s there at the very end as a motorist asking Randy Travis for directions. It is a supposedly comic scene, but Reilly mugs it up, and the writing is sub-sitcom level. It falls entirely flat, which I suppose is appropriate, considering the mess of a movie preceding it.

I'll have to say, I did feel some nostalgic warmth watching the scenes that depict the crew hanging out, eating or working together in a western setting. Those scenes felt honest to me. Undoubtedly the crew depicted are played by the actual crew making this film, and you can feel their bond, all sharing their efforts for a common work. I worked a lot in transportation for movie companies shooting in Tucson, Arizona in the late 1980s. Many of them were westerns. It all looked so nostalgically familiar to me. Now, I realize that these moments are only going to be resonant for myself, or for others who may have similar memories, and are not really a fair recommendation for sitting through this pointless effort.

Of all the guest performers in the film, Burt Reynolds is given the most to do, and has by far the best moments of the entire production. He exudes his usual presence and charm in every scene in which he appears. But he could do that just by showing up. At one point he walks across the prairie with the young boy (called only The Kid) - who, beyond all logic, has landed a major role in the film – and gives him some acting advice. "Never let them catch you acting," he says to the boy. I don't know if the line was scripted, or if it was an ad-lib on Reynold's part, but for me it really summed up the kind of honest integrity in the best of Burt's work. Plus, it's just damn good advice for any actor, poetically placed inside of a nutshell.

–Ron Ford

Walker, Texas Ranger (1993 – 2001)

Walker, Texas Ranger is a feelgood television show that is a throwback to an era of simpler times. There seems to be always some sort of lesson that is taught but it is not obvious until the story ends. Chuck Norris stars as Texas Ranger Cordell Walker, a decorated former Marine and Vietnam Veteran turned famed Texas Ranger. He is half Cherokee and lived with his parents until they were murdered by drunk fair goers who did not like the fact that Walker's white mother was with his Cherokee father. He was left angry and bitter at the world, often fighting with other children at orphanages until his father's brother, Ray was located. His first day on the reservation also saw him fighting with two local boys, who marveled at his courage trying to fight them both. His Uncle Ray mentioned that he would need this courage to deal with what would come from being half Cherokee. This is a theme that runs through the next nine years of programming.

The initial pilots for the series were three official episodes but the first episode, "One Riot, One Ranger," which introduced Walker to new Assistant District Attorney Alexandra Cahill was two hours long. This is the underpinning of the series, introducing a relationship that not only shapes Walker himself, but the tone of the program. In subsequent airings, it is listed as two different episodes. There is an initial disdain, if not outright dislike between Alex and Walker. She finds him as arrogant and boastful when trying a case in which he took down several criminals at one time and handcuffed them to the running bar of his truck. So, when on examination he quips something to the effect of, "You ever hear the saying, one riot, one ranger?" She doesn't believe him, so he finally asks the men on trial who arrested them. Their response was basically, 'You did, Ranger.' Walker is also partnered with someone new after working for some time with a now-retired Texas Ranger, C. D. Parker. Walker and C. D. got along well, they were both old school style, easy going cowboys. Unfortunately for Walker, he would be paired up with a younger, and his polar opposite, James Trivette. Even though Jimmy played for the Dallas Cowboys he is still very much a Baltimore, Maryland boy. He's also a little bit of a tech nerd (in 1993) wanting the newest devices that he believes will make police work easier as opposed to Walker's style of beating the streets. As the series progresses the four primary characters become very much family: even Jimmy and C.D. enjoy a teasing, fraternal relationship.

Alex and Walker do not begin to bond until she begins being stalked in the second episode of the pilot. The problem is Alex can't prove who is stalking her and Walker shows faith in her fears by looking out for her. The stalker goes so far as to kill Alex's beloved horse. Walker shows that he has a heart when he gifts Alex the foal that one of his mares delivers.

Almost immediately, little snippets of Walker's past are shown as he relies heavily on the lessons Uncle Ray began to teach him as a child, but we do not get a full episode that mentions life after he left the reservation until the final episode of the test run. We learn about Walker's training in the martial arts when his friend Yoshi shows up. Yoshi's father is the man who taught Walker martial arts, but it has been ten years since Walker has last heard from Yoshi. A powerful member of the Yakuza has been killed and Walker is suspicious when he learns that Yoshi is a member of the Japanese crime family. The truth is that Yoshi is not the bad guy and was trying to reclaim stolen Japanese art.

This sets up the first official season in which Walker proves that he is willing to listen to criminals or others when they have been wrongly accused. Perhaps it is his Cherokee senses that allow him to tell when a person is telling the truth or when something is wrong. For example, a bank robber who is arrested for a crime that he did not commit, but due to the fact that he does have a criminal record, an insane bounty hunter is hell bent on getting him by any means necessary. He is even willing to try and kill the bank robber's brother just to draw him out.

Another time and in another episode, a parolee named Billy that Walker had mentored is missing. He learns during the episode that the reason Billy has gone missing is because he is being forced to commit crimes under duress. His parole officer has kidnapped Billy's wife and young son to force him to commit the crimes.

Season Two begins to show heavier and darker themes than the previous one. Walker and Trivette are in Midland, Texas to track down an escaped convict named Harris. On their drive back to Dallas, they stop in the small town of Adelaide for the night. The sheriff of the town used to be with Department of Public Service when Walker was, and he is happy to put their prisoner up for the night. They are then met by Mr. and Mrs. Mays, a black family who are concerned with their son who was arrested because he argued with deputies in the town, who refused to allow the family to eat in the restaurant because they were black. Jimmy pretends to be the teenager's cousin to bail him out and makes a show of calling Walker a cousin too. When Jimmy escorts him out, the sheriff, Langley, no longer hides his disgust and tells Walker, "Is this what the Rangers have come too?" Whether or not Walker, at this time, recognizes him as a racist, he answers honestly, "I hope so because he's one hell of a partner....and besides he actually passed his Ranger test which is more than you did."

Racism is heavy in this episode with the two comparing experiences of having racists target them, the difference is that it still bothers Jimmy because he is still confronted with it every day because of his color, whereas Walker is lighter and takes after his mother. The truth of the character Walker is that he may not look the part of a Cherokee, he still feels the pain of racism everyday as it was racists that cost him the life of his parents. This leads to Jimmy not waiting for Walker when he realizes that young B. J. Mays has gone back to Adelaide, thinking that he can confront the sheriff and get their money back. He does leave word with C. D. to let him track down Walker for him with the message of where he is going and why, trusting Walker to recognize the seriousness of the situation. Walker proves that he has Jimmy's back and that the villains will always be dumb enough to think he's only dangerous with his gun. In this case he is exceptionally rough with those he fights, and he shows his moral outrage/disgust by removing Langley's badge before sneering his under arrest.

As each season progresses the storylines are filled with more examples of how much Walker cares about people and the seriousness of his fight scenes are amped up when its somebody he considers family or someone like a child who cannot protect themselves is at risk.

As a tie into his appearance at WWF's *Survivor Series* in 1994, coinciding with the official second season of Walker, many professional wrestlers and fighters began making cameos on *Walker*. The wrestlers did not even have to be regulars on WWF television either, in fact, most of the wrestlers were all working for WCW at the time of their appearances. Some of the biggest names in wrestling of all time made cameos, "Macho Man" Randy Savage, Hulk Hogan, and a two-part episode starring "Rowdy" Roddy Piper, who coincidently played a professional wrestler, a man estranged from his family due to his love of wrestling. His wife had seen a murder and was on the run. Just when Piper bonds with the kid and realizes he's sick he tries to push him away, which of course makes the kid run away. Piper and Walker must team up to rescue the kid.

My personal favorite episode is in two parts and features Haley Joel Osmet in the sixth season entitled "Lucas." Not only does it feature a child prominently that Walker is compelled to protect, but it delves into Walker's own feelings about having been an orphan himself. In a series of stories to help ease Lucas missing his mother, he tells of his life on the reservation, and to teach Lucas about being a Cherokee. Eventually, Walker has to break it to the very small, neglected child that the boy has AIDS from his drug-using mother. The nightmares that Lucas has are similar to things that happened to Walker as a child (without the autoimmune issue). Lucas' boogie man, though, is his mom's boyfriend, a career criminal who regularly physically abused and kept his mother high, so she did not realize that he kept Lucas locked in a closet, starving and covered in his own filth when he was found. Walker, Jimmy, C. D., and Alex all fell in love with Lucas who Walker took from the orphanage after learning the other kids refused to play with him because the older kids heard the staff talking. They bullied the younger kids with scary stories that if they were friends with Lucas or played with him, they'd catch AIDS and die.

The moral of this episode was one of servant leadership as Lucas wanted to go to schools and talk about how he had AIDS, demystifying it. He wanted people to know that being friends with someone didn't mean you'd catch it. When Alex asked him about a birthday party, she found out that he had never had a party before, and she almost broke down in tears to assure him that he'd have one this year. The guests were late, and the adults were worried no one would show up. One of the fathers admitted that he and the other parents were planning on not coming till their children educated them about how being friends with someone didn't mean you'd get AIDS. The father admitted to being foolish and Lucas got his big party.

This is also a perfect example of how Walker gets when a child or family member is threatened. Lucas' reoccurring nightmare was his mother's boyfriend, Rayford Cobb, coming after him. In order to help him with this nightmare and overwhelming fear, Walker's solution was to take him to the Cherokee Reservation he grew up on to meet with a spiritual leader, White Eagle. They had a sweat lodge ceremony, and Lucas was encouraged to 'see' that Walker was there to help him fight Cobb off. Emboldened, Lucas went after the spectral visage of Cobb with a tomahawk echoing the same kind of voraciousness that Walker would visit upon Cobb in the real take down.

This is one episode that I was heavily invested in and, despite the fact the show is aired on channels known for religious programming, I was able to suspend reality enough to cheer Walker on and to curse Cobb like the low-down dog he was written to be. This is an episode that you get to see a different side of Walker. Over the course of nine seasons, you get accustomed to the fact that Walker, like Chuck Norris in real life, is a bad ass. This episode, as in the final episodes of season nine when Walker and Alex have their daughter, Angel, you get to see the range of Norris' ability to act. He shows a real depth of emotion and vulnerability as he has to eulogize Lucas, burying him in their shared favorite spot on the ranch. In Season Nine, he has to worry about the health and safety of Alex and their daughter when the baby is in distress. This is the first time, I remember, a hint of Norris' religious belief is infused with Walker's Cherokee mysticism. Although, Walker and Alex's friendship with clergy, including Walker's student, Trent's father, Thunder, among others is scattered throughout the series.

Taking a stab at nine seasons of a beloved television show in a couple of thousand words is difficult but, luckily, *Walker, Texas Ranger* wasn't complex enough to provide multiple intricate scenarios and convoluted plotlines. At its core, it is about a man that thinks that justice means more than an arrest or putting the bad guy away. In a strange way, even for the time period, *Walker, Texas Ranger* is about equity. Not equality, but real equity where people get what they need and not what the world thinks they need. Except Cordell Walker, sadly. I am loathe to compare this to a Shakespearean tragedy and am not even sure that Norris and the producers did this on purpose, but Walker's journey is as much about his unhappiness as it is about making sure the bad guys pay.

–Kristina Stancil

Walker, Texas Ranger: The Themes (1993 – 2001)

I'm a musician and composer, and some of my favorite composition projects have been theme music projects because they present a unique writing challenge. Writing a good theme for a show seems as simple as writing a catchy tune, but it's really a very difficult thing to do well. The theme music needs to set the stage for what viewers should expect to see, and in a very short amount of time - most themes are between 30 seconds and one minute in length. Composers use specific instrument sounds or whole musical styles to evoke a time period or a place, such as the bellicose drums and sweeping orchestral string sounds of the *Game of Thrones* theme or the bright 90's pop of the Rembrandts in the *Friends* theme. It's all there to prepare you, the viewer, for what you're about to see.

A show no less epic as CBS's Chuck Norris star vehicle *Walker, Texas Ranger* required not one, not two, but *three* different theme songs to fully crystallize its awesomeness into its purest form. In this essay, I'll be doing a musicological analysis pointing out the outstanding features of each theme and rating it on its awesomeness on a scale of 0-10.

Theme 1 - Season 1: The inaugural theme for the *Walker* series is a fairly boilerplate 80's cop show theme, which wouldn't have been out of place on a show like Hunter or MacGyver. It wouldn't surprise me if it was in composer Tirk Wilder's library for years when the show entered production. The only real nod to the show's "modern cowboy" theme is the short blast of fake synthesized harmonica courtesy of the E-MU Proteus 1, a very popular synthesizer sound module of the early 90's - probably added to the song just before submitting it to be used in the show. Of special note are the badly timed sound effects to match the images in the title montage; my personal favorite is the "hitting a side of beef with a two-by-four" sound effect accompanying Chuck's roundhouse kick over Floyd "Red Crow" Westerman's title card. Perfectly competent, but nothing special. 6/10 cowboy hats for this version.

Theme 2 - Season 2: *Walker*'s first season is a success, apparently so much so that they bring veteran TV composer Jerrold Immel (*Dallas, Voyagers!*) on board to compose a NEW theme for the show. Too bad that he thought that he was writing music for a show set in the Amazon Rainforest, or at least that what the semi-tribal drum patterns and synth pan flute (once again from our good friend the E-MU Proteus, or possibly it's early-90's cousin the Korg M1) seem to suggest. This theme must not have pleased Mr. Norris either, because it was roundhouse-kicked out of the show after episode 11. Sorry Jerrold, maybe the Rainforest Cafe is looking for some background music. 3/10 Eyes of the Ranger for this version.

Theme 3 - Season 2 and Beyond: Speaking of the eyes of the ranger… original composer Tirk Wilder makes a stunning return with the song "The Eyes of the Ranger" in episode 12 of Season 2, which includes a vocal from the show's star, Chuck Norris. Chuck's dull and unremarkable vocal performance prefigures the "insurance salesman with a studio in his basement" sound by at least a decade. In his half-season away from the show, Tirk Wilder came up with a much more representative composition for the show's tone and setting. Featuring a twangy low baritone guitar (possibly courtesy of the new Roland JV series synthesizers) and a choogling train beat, it's antiseptic version of outlaw country music paints a Southwestern motif with the same grit and authenticity as the Navajo blanket and buffalo horns that hang over the lobby fireplace of the Albuquerque Marriott Inn. In other words, a perfect match. 10/10 karate kicks.

The third time was the charm, as "Eyes of the Ranger" not only connected with viewers but inspired cover versions - my favorite by a Russian cowboy named Aleksander Obukhov, which can be found on YouTube. So, when you're in Volgoglad or Belgorad, look behind you - because that's where the Ranger's gonna be.

–Daryl Bean

WWF Survivor Series (1994)

There was not much buildup to Chuck Norris' appearance at World Wrestling Federation's *Survivor Series* in November 1994. It was live from San Antonio, Texas from the Freeman Coliseum. *Walker, Texas Ranger* was already a hit series further cementing Norris' status as a bona fide action star. It was in its second season and was different that the other procedural cop shows.

Throughout the night many of the heel or bad guy wrestlers like Tantanka and Bam-Bam Bigelow scoffed at the idea of Chuck Norris being the special guest referee for the main event casket match between Undertaker and Yokozuna. They both boasted that they were not afraid of the martial arts legend. Tantanka and Bam-Bam were two of the wrestlers who had interfered in Yokozuna and Taker's match in January at the *Royal Rumble*. Yet Tantanka steered clear of the ring.

During the main event, Chuck was billed as "Texas' own," and was given a standing ovation from the capacity crowd in San Antonio. Vince hailed him as a martial arts legend and a certified box office star. He high fived the fans as he came to the ring and saluted the fans as he climbed into the ring. Like most major wrestling events of the time, he was hailed with a shower of pyro benefiting his status as a special star and was billed by commentator Vince McMahon as a special trouble shooting referee and martial arts expert extraordinaire.

As the match went on, Vince McMahon and Gorilla Monsoon wondered if anyone would be gutsy enough to test the skills of Chuck Norris. In fact, the late Yokozuna (cousin of current WWE champion Roman Reigns and Dwayne "The Rock" Johnson) was knocked to the outside of the ring. As he quickly crawled off the casket, he realized that Chuck was behind him and stumbled away from him warily, despite the fact he was a former sumo wrestler, weighing in excess of six hundred pounds. Despite his size, he wasn't willing to push his luck.

For those who don't know, an appearance at a major WWE pay-per-view by the Undertaker is an ominous and creepy theatric experience that never fails to incite a wrestling audience. As with the arrival of Chuck Norris, the fans rose with respect. He, however, was not distracted by the theatrics, but seemed amused by the reaction that the fans and Yokozuna had as a very large casket was wheeled to the ringside area. Vince and Gorilla called Yokozuna's reaction to both Chuck and The Undertaker as paranoia.

Chuck stayed primarily focused on the backstage area, shaking his head in amusement at the reaction of the fans. Every once in a while, the camera would focus on Chuck as the commentary centered on who would be gutsy enough to try him. With about ten minutes until the end of the pay per view, King Kong Bundy and Bam-Bam Bigelow started down to the ringside area but neither risked taking Chuck on. They were only there to serve as a distraction because Irwin R. Shyster, (father of former WWE superstar Bray Wyatt) came in to attack The Undertaker behind Chuck's back. The full time WWE referees that were on hand to call the match were also distracted.

Once that plan backfired and the match progressed, Jeff Jarrett, closer in size to Chuck Norris, decided that he was going to confront the legend. He hesitated briefly but then he stepped forward and whatever he said to Chuck, resulted in a stick side kick. Jarrett's antics and the force of the side kick sent him flying head over heels. He gets up and briefly considers going back for a second shot, but once he realizes that Chuck is still watching him, unfazed, he shifts direction. He quickly runs off. As the match ended the camera focused on Chuck smiling in amusement as good triumphant over evil, much the same way that things happened on *Walker, Texas Ranger.*

On the following episode of *WWF Raw*, they discussed Chuck being a part of the pay per view. Vince McMahon was joined by legendary wrestler, Jerry "The King" Lawler on commentary. They discussed the match between Yokozuna and The Undertaker and Lawler claimed that Chuck defending himself from Jarrett's aggression was a cheap shot. Vince scoffed at him since Chuck's being at *Survivor Series* was specifically to keep people from getting involved in the match. They later showed stills and recapped the match. Vince highlighted the fact that Chuck held off super heavyweights Bam-Bam Bigelow and King Kong Bundy. Lawler discredited Chuck taking out Jarrett while Vince admonished the heel announcer's tactic. Fans of Chuck Norris know that if there is one thing that he cannot stand, it is a bully.

–Kristina Stancil

Hellbound (1994)

Hellbound (1994) was the last film Chuck Norris and his kid brother Aaron made for Cannon Group. In fact, it was the last film anybody made for Cannon Group. The company filed for bankruptcy shortly afterwards. I'm not saying *Hellbound* was the reason for that, but I will say it was the last rusty nail in the coffin.

This is the only Norris film with supernatural underpinnings. We are alerted to that right up front with a *Star Wars*-style prologue that crawls up the screen and tapers away into the distance. Here we learn of Satan's emissary, Prosatanos, who seeks to bring about Armageddon.

Prosatanos, as far as I could find, is not a demon mentioned in any actual Christian or Hebrew scriptures. It is, however, the name of a German metal band and a character from *World of Warcraft*.

The movie starts out somewhat promisingly in 1186 A.D. with decent period detail and costumes, and scads of mounted extras as nights. King Richard the Lionhearted (David Robb) and his holy crusaders stop Prosatanos (Christopher Neame) from sacrificing a young prince. They seal him into a stone sarcophagus. Lionheart chops his magic scepter (the source of his power) into nine pieces, which are hidden in nine locations around the world.

Then we cut to 1951 where two grave robbers break into the tomb and unwittingly release Prosatanos. They do not survive.

Chicago, 1994. We meet Shatter (Norris) and Jackson (Calvin Levels), two police detectives tracking down a drug dealer to a ratty downtown hotel. Meanwhile, coincidentally, in the same hotel, Prosatanos is fucking a giggly, annoying hooker (Zoe Trilling). Even demons have their needs.

While the hooker showers, Rabbi Mordecai Schindler (Ori Levy) arrives, with what appears to be the crown of the scepter. But the Rabbi double crosses Prosatanos and stabs him with a ceremonial dagger. But it takes more than a knife in the heart to take down the Evil One. He plucks out the Rabbi's heart and shows it to him in an all-too-familiar gag. The hooker comes out of the bathroom and witnesses the destruction. Prosatanos tosses her out of the window and, as fate would have it, she lands right on Shatter and Jackson's car.

Their first encounter with Prosantos does not go well. "I shot a guy in the chest – twice – and he still kicked the shit out of me," Shatter says to Jackson after Prosatanos flees. But they retrieve what appears to be the head of the scepter from the crime scene, as well as a business card for Rinehart Krieger, an antiques dealer in Israel. Penciled on the back is the name of a Professor Lockley at Mathers University.

At the university they learn from the professor's assistant, Leslie Hawkins (Sheree J. Wilson), that Lockley is in Israel. Shatter instantly has the hots for Leslie, and she for him. She identifies the artifact as the crown of Prosatanos' scepter.

Ina very unlikely development, the cops are sent to Israel to escort the Rabbi's corpse home and to be questioned by Jerusalem police, which apparently can't be done over the phone.

At Jerusalem University, looking for Professor Lockley, they run into Leslie Hawkins, who takes them to an excavation site to meet Lockley. He turns out to be – Prosatanos! He refers to her as Princess. He is very brusque with the cops and calls their artifact a fake.

Later, Jackson is hit from behind by antiques dealer Rinehart Krieger, who steals the artifact. He is later confronted by Prosatanos, who has hired him to get the artifact. But it is a fake. He is killed.

At the crime scene, Jackson finds a scroll with nine names, all scratched off but one.

They go to an ancient ruin in search of the last remaining name, a monk named Farouk (Shabtai Konorti), who explains that Prosatanos needs all the pieces of the scepter and a sacrifice of royal blood to bring about Armageddon. After the cops have left, Prosatanos arrives and kills Farouk, retrieving the actual scepter crown.

Meanwhile, Prosatanos reveals his identity to Leslie and kidnaps her. The cops learn that she is the daughter of one Duke Claymore. She has royal blood coursing through her veins.

They return to the excavation site and rescue Leslie, who tells them how to kill Prosatanos. The evil one appears. They fight (slow-motion round-house kicks) and he reverts to demon form in a very average prosthetic makeup before he is dispatched by our hero.

Shatter gets the girl and they return to the states.

Though it pretends to be a demonic thriller, this is a typical Norris vehicle at heart. Little brother Aaron's direction is efficient but uninspired. In a horror film, we would have seen the various slayings around the world as Prosatanos collected the pieces of his scepter. Here we follow the cops in a standard detective plot. We only learn of all those murders when they do - it is just another clue on the way to the preordained conclusion.

There are a few elements that set it apart, however. Firstly, the well-produced opening medieval sequence. It offered nothing new, but was unexpected eye-candy. Secondly, Norris's partner was not killed, which is usually *de rigueur* in buddy cop movies. Perhaps they were hoping for a sequel before Cannon Group split the sheets. Thirdly, the Israeli setting gives it a different look than most of these films and makes for some very interesting locations.

But the most unusual (and unpleasant) element of the film is Shatter's relationship with his partner, Jackson. Shatter gets the girl and thwarts the bad guy and hits all those action hero notes, but he remains unlikeable because he treats Jackson like an underling who isn't worthy of the post. He plays tricks on him, keeps facts from him, and smirks at him behind his back. The fact that Jackson is Black and Norris is white gives it all a very uncomfortable feel that was, at the very least, poorly thought through.

–Ron Ford

Top Dog (1995)

Before you sit down to watch *Top Dog*, you have to answer yourself one important question: *How much disbelief can I suspend?*

Top Dog was released in 1995, six years after 1989 and the duo of cop/dog buddy films *Turner and Hooch* with Tom Hanks and *K9* with Jim Belushi. *Top Dog* follows the formula pretty closely — canine is teamed up with non-canine trained police officer, wackiness ensues, crime is solved.

The problem is that there really isn't all that much wackiness. There are some incongruities. There are some really annoying things to nitpick over. There are even some attempts at humor, but most of these fall flat.

Top Dog begins with a group of white nationalists, you know, like most films aimed at kids do. Reportedly, this was because actor Chuck Norris and his brother director and co-writer Aaron Norris, wanted the film to have a message about racial unity and thought that having the villains be neo-Nazi domestic terrorists would be a great way to showcase this.

The basic premise of the film is that super canine cop Reno and his partner are both shot while investigating the aftermath of a building explosion and fire. This scene provides our first look at a couple of themes which will run throughout the film:

Blatant disregard for the law on the part of law enforcement.

Everyone is completely inept at their jobs.

The occasional exception to the previous statement is Reno the dog.

Lou, Reno's original partner, and Reno respond to a building fire. The apartment complex is in engulfed in flames, but the fire department and other patrol officers are on the scene. Lou volunteers to "help" and proceeds to enter the building despite the fact that there are trained professionals their in the appropriate gear. We learn that there is a baby still in the building, but none of the fire department individuals can find it. Reno saves the baby, of course.

Lou then notices two men in a crowd and recalls that someone described two men running from the building. They follow these two men (who none of the other police officers noticed) to a docked ship. They sneak aboard that night, without a warrant or even calling in to let the Desk Sargent know where they are. They break into a number of crates, finding explosives and guns. The owner of the boat shoots them both and leaves them for dead.

A *month* later, a hung-over Jake Wilder (Norris) is called by his captain. He wants him to report to duty despite the fact that he is on suspension. Lou's death is mentioned numerous times, plus, when we see Reno again he is completely healed from his gunshot wound. The captain partners Jake, who "only works alone" with the dog. This scene does feature an amusing bit where the captain has the files of Jake and Reno and noticed the number of commonalities, right down to the number of commendations and how many times they have been shot. We also get another of the incongruities as it appears that Jake is the only person on the police force who doesn't know who Reno is. Maybe it's because he works alone.

We transition to the K9 training course where we see Reno take down a training officer and find drugs. We also see that there is actually a K9 unit with officers trained to work with dogs, so why they team Jake with Reno is a continuing mystery. We return to Jake's pigpen of a house and Reno runs away to hide in the car.

We should probably note that the fact that Reno, played by Digby and Betty (Betty was also featured in the 1993 film *Dennis the Menace*) is a Briard, which might seem odd to some people. Briards are, in fact, used by some police departments, but primarily as search and rescue and tracking jobs and occasionally as therapy dogs for those suffering from PTSD. The choice was a conscious one, as the film makers wanted a dog with a slightly comedic look, but which would still possess the size and strength to take down a full-grown man.

From here on out, the film alternates between serious scenes, primarily gun fights and martial arts, and attempts at comedy. The police stand around one house waiting for a drug sniffing dog without clearing the house which has a giant biker hiding in the closet. Jake helps his mom with her gardening while the kid (because of course there is a kid) takes Reno to a "dog show." Note: both Jake and Reno are supposed to be on duty at this time. Also, the person who wrote this has never been to a dog show where dogs are rated on how closely they match their breed standards, not on "poise" and "grooming."

Fortunately, Jake's mom is smarter than the police, the sheriff's office, and the FBI, because she manages to figure out that the white supremacists might be planning something on Hitler's birthday — the following day. They also don't think that the "Coalition for Racial Unity" might be a prime target, but that's a little later.

Jake and Reno go to the villain's hideout, where a pair of officers are sitting in an unmarked car, and we get this exchange:

Jake: You got the warrant?

Detective: It didn't come through.

Jake: What do you mean it didn't come through?

Detective: I don't know Jake, they said something about probable cause.

Jake: I'm going in anyway. If I'm not back in 20 minutes, call for back-up."

Jake finds a notebook with all of the terrorists' targets. Reno escapes with it while Jake does some martial arts. He gets captured, but Reno helps him escape. Guns are shot. People are kicked. Reno knocks people off of balconies. They stop the bombing and there is a final stab at humor.

Top Dog suffers from serious personality disorder when it comes to tone, as mentioned above. This also translates to the score which features circus music during one of the gun battles, Cajun music during the dog show, and a blues song followed by more Cajun music during the closing credits. The dubbing for the dog is absolutely atrocious. Growls, whines, sniffing, and barking all occur when the dog is obviously being silent. This is loud enough to be really distracting.

Still, we can forgive some of this because it's a kid's movie, right? Surely it did OK at the box office? I mean, Norris was fresh off of *Sidekicks*, another movie aimed at a younger audience.

Top Dog, the movie featuring a white supremacists plot to blow up a number of buildings was released nine days after the bombing of the Alfred P. Murrah Federal Building in Oklahoma City.

–Michael Cieslak

Forest Warrior (1996)

When I was a kid, I thought Chuck Norris was pretty awesome. Myself and one of my friends used to watch stuff like *Good Guys Wear Black* and *Lone Wolf McQuade*. We went to the theater to watch *Delta Force*. I had an *Invasion USA* one-sheet hanging in my room. In my mind, Chuck Norris was pure cinematic gold. But then somewhere along the way those movies I loved made way for straight-to-video shit like *Forest Warrior*. The title, the artwork, and the trailer all made me think it was going to be completely awful. And I was right, but somehow the film turned out to be even worse than I had anticipated. Most of Norris' "better" films were made by Cannon Films, who were a film company known for making trash like *Superman IV: The Quest for Peace* and scores of old man Charles Bronson movies. Cannon was already defunct by the time *Forest Warrior* came out, but I doubt they would have distributed this. That's right, *Forest Warrior* is beneath Cannon Films standards.

Let's start with the plot. Chuck Norris plays the ghost of a mountain man who was attacked by cut-throats while trekking across through the forest to obtain medicine for his sickly squaw wife back in 1875. After being killed, his body was discovered by a bear (complete with shitty bear POV shots) and its animal buddies who then used animal magic to resurrect him as some sort of supernatural being whose sole reason for existence is to "protect the mountain and everyone who loved it." If that sounds horrible (and it is), just wait... After Norris' character, Jedediah McKenna, was resurrected, he possessed the ability to transform into three different animals—a bear, a wolf, and an eagle. As it is explained in the film, "The bear, the wolf, and the eagle became one in McKenna." He also possesses the power to look into a person's eyes and peer into their soul.

All of the children in the nearby town know the legend of the Forest Warrior, but no one really believes it. For decades, groups of the town's children have traipsed around the woods, discovering what is essentially a giant, elaborately constructed tree house. Apparently, this is the Forest Warrior's home, although the film doesn't go much into that, and the Forest Warrior never seems to be hanging out there. Despite their not believing the legend, the kids all play on the thing without anyone ever questioning why the hell it's there.

Near the beginning of the film, we learn that an evil lumber man from town named Travis Thorn has plans to cut down all the trees in the forest. Most of the town is against the idea since no one stands to gain anything from the cutting of the trees but Thorn. Instead of waiting on a court decision, Thorn moves forward with his diabolical tree-cutting plot. (And yes, again, this film and its plot suck.) Along the way, not only the trees, but also various children from town are put in harm's way, so it is up to the Forest Warrior to restore peace. How does he do this, you might ask. If you have ever seen the meme of Chuck Norris stopping the moving blade of a chainsaw with his bare hand, well... that image is from this turd of a movie. The Forest Warrior also beats on baddies with a fighting technique that is said to be Native American but is clearly a combination of traditional martial arts.

The movie is directed by Norris' brother, Aaron, and written by Ron Swanson (not the cool Nick Offerman Ron Swanson character from *Parks and Rec*, but the one who also wrote a bunch of other crummy Chuck Norris stuff like *Top Dog*). Watching this, one gets the distinct impression that the story was designed to work around Norris' inability to act, as well as to limit the number of days Norris had to be on set. Despite Norris being the titular character, he doesn't show up all that much and when he does, he just looks stoic and delivers a couple of lines. Maybe the idea was to hide the fact that Norris is a crappy actor, but this doesn't work; such is the genius of Norris the thespian, who can display horrible acting chops by simply doing nothing. However, because of his limited screen time and dialogue, his crappiness is subdued here.

Some of the acting in the film is fairly decent. Journeyman actor Roscoe Lee Brown gives the film's finest performance. I cannot find one criticism to make of his performance as the town's seemingly lone black man. *Barney Miller* alum Max Gail is pretty good, as are veteran actors Terry Kiser and Loretta Switt. The truth is, these actors' performances are occasionally slightly cartoony, but the blame for that seems to fall more on the shoulders of the director and screenwriters. Switt really has nothing to do here. The only thing notable about her appearance is that the hairstyle she sports here is beyond bad. So bad in fact that it threatens to wipe out any fond memories you might have of her *MASH* character "Hot Lips" Houlihan. The only really, truly godawful bad performance in the film is delivered by Michael Beck, who plays an alcoholic father. Beck is decent in other films, such as *Xanadu* and *The Warriors*, but here he is embarrassingly awful. It was almost like Beck did some method acting by getting really drunk to play the role and then got so drunk that he could no longer adequately play a drunk. Half the cast of the film is comprised of 12-year-old children, and all of them out-act him by a country mile.

There isn't anything positive to report about this movie other than it is having good intentions about saving the environment, but you know the saying about the road to hell being paved with good intentions... This movie is hell.

–Andrew J. Rausch

Logan's War: Bound by Honor (1998)

I am not gonna mince words. If there is such a thing as a Hallmark action movie, this is it. You could use that frame of reference and probably write a comparable movie with your imagination; couple the Afterschool Special dialogue with several over the top gritty action sequences and you have a general idea of the tone of *Logan's War: Bound by Honor*. The *Reader's Digest* plot synopsis is that an Army Ranger takes on a mob gang. The reality of the film is not nearly so simple (or as preposterous).

Chuck plays Logan's uncle, the heroically named Jake Fallon. Jake is, of course, a former Green Beret (who obviously earned a Distinguished Service Cross) who takes lil' Logan in after Logan's entire family is killed. Logan sort of had a premonition and had tried to tell his dad that the fam was in danger, but to no avail. He did successfully manage to hide when the mob came in and slaughtered everyone else (a BIT jarring for a TV movie that started with such a cornball, well, Hallmark feel), and when he is shipped off to Uncle Chuck, it becomes apparent that Chuckie also has whatever weird psychic power Logan has displayed. This sounds way cooler than it really is.

Logan's grandfather Ben (James Gammon, in easily the best and most ably played role) also lives on the ranch, and he and Jake discover the child's penchant for perceiving impending danger together. This setup is shown in just a few minutes, really – Jake initially fights against them (kinda) about eating and living on the ranch, but that angst that is born of watching the mob kill his whole family lasts about 30 seconds. Somewhere in this time period, Logan tells Jake he's gonna kill the dude who called for that hit, which leads to a pretty amusing montage where Chuck is teaching the kid how to whoop some serious Chuck Norris style ass.

Then BOOM, Logan is an adult (played by the extremely rom-comish Eddie Cibrian) and, of course, follows in Jake's footsteps as a Green Beret. The rest goes down exactly how you would think it would, even based solely on the Hallmarkian action info I gave you at the beginning. The script, written by Chuck and his brother Aaron (which is pretty neat, I think), is standard and by the book, but the protagonists (especially Ben) are all amiable enough to be...let's be complimentary here and say *adequate* for what they're doing.

I admit, I'm not entirely sure how big an audience there is for a Hallmark action movie. Maybe there is a huge crowd clamoring for such things. Maybe in the nineties that was a thing and I just didn't notice because I was watching *Scream* and *Clerks* and listening to grunge. I am NOT among the alleged group who might find this movie appealing, and as such I feel kinda bad about commenting so negatively about it, because for all I know this is the *Citizen Kane* of Hallmark action movies and hits every longed after note. I suspect this isn't the truth, though, and I'll give a reason why.

The reason is good ol' Chuck himself. Now, I LIKE Chuck Norris movies. Well, I like *some* Chuck Norris movies.

Fine, I like *Firewalker* and probably *Missing in Action*, though I haven't seen either one since the days when I would walk into Jumbo Video and rent stuff like *Commando* and *Cobra*. That was a long time ago. But I do remember really enjoying *Firewalker* in particular and that film carried me over to a generally good feeling about our hero the Chuckster.

I loved the *Chuck Norris and the Karate Kommandos* cartoon when I was a kid, and I especially loved the short-lived Marvel comics, which were under the beloved STAR imprint and lasted for, I don't know, maybe four issues. That's a guess. I had three or four and I read them cover to cover dozens of times. But I ain't gonna look it up. For all I know, they're still publishing that comic and there are hundreds of them. But I think three or four is a pretty safe guess.

Taking all that into consideration, please realize that it doesn't give me any great pleasure to report that the esteemed Mr. Norris is…let's take the high road again and say, *not* the best thing about this movie. He isn't abysmal or absolutely irredeemable, though. There are plenty of harmless scenes of Chuck standing in fields looking stoic and staring off thoughtfully into nature's soul. There are a few sequences that suggest he still had plenty of martial arts chutzpah in the late nineties.

But the problems come when he has, well, dialogue.

To elaborate, and I plead with you all not to tell Chuck that I sort of talked junk about him, because I do still hold a general feeling of affection for him. Ok, and I'm still plenty scared of him even though he is eighty years old. But it must be said: *Logan's War* finds him struggling to find an emotional base; or more accurately, it seems as though he learned to emote RIGHT before they shot the movie ("A smile signifies happiness…curl the corners of your mouth up. Yes, *kind of* like that"). He also seems to have been taught how to convincingly mimic eating right before they rolled film. "Chuck, this is a fork…when you put it to your face, you open your mouth and take stuff off of it."

And yes, this is understandable! After all, Chuck Norris doesn't *need* mortal sustenance in the same way that mere humans do. He doesn't have to actually FEEL feelings and needs them described to him every once in a while.

He eats bullets for breakfast and shits out gun powder before bedtime and in between he sucks nutrients from thin air and karate kicks any negativity away like it was a foreboding vision of a smirking Steven Seagal hulking over the production craft table hungrily looking for Chuck's scraps.

–Paul Counelis

Sons of Thunder (1999)

Episodes with Chuck Norris: Thunder by Your Side (Apr. 17, 1999), Lost & Found (Apr. 3, 1999), Fighting Back (March, 13, 1999), Moment of Truth (March, 6, 1999). Episodes without Chuck Norris: Daddy's Girl (March 20, 1999), Underground (Apr. 10, 1999).

The series ran for six episodes in 1999 but had a back-door pilot in 1997 in the Season Five episode of *Walker, Texas Ranger* that was titled "Sons of Thunder." Characters from the series popped up repeatedly on *Walker* before and after *Sons of Thunder* was cancelled. Chuck Norris and his brother Aaron served as the creators and producers of the series and Chuck Norris also appeared in small parts in four of the six episodes of the entire run.

Norris was so popular at the time for playing Texas Ranger Cordell Walker that he was the third billing on the posters promoting this show, despite not technically being a full-time cast member.

Sheree J. Wilson also appeared in three of the episodes that Norris was in, she played his longtime friend, girlfriend and later wife on *Walker, Texas Ranger*, and was also a prosecuting attorney in the area where both shows are set. The following episodes feature Chuck:

"Moment of Truth" - The series premier shows Carlos make a mistake while tracking a killer, resulting in the death of his partner. After his captain tried to take him off the case, he resigned from the Dallas Police Department and got the help of his friend Trent Malloy to help solve the case. This results in them opening a private detective agency called "Sons of Thunder."

Chuck Norris is barely in the episode, most notably teaching Trent to use throwing stars in one scene.

"Fighting Back" - Forced to go undercover to solve a series of computer thefts at a factory, Carlos and Trent pose as ex-cons. Walker barely appears in the episode, but Alex Cahill has a part in the b-story where Trent and Carlos are helping a woman who was beaten and raped. Alex helps the woman overcome her fears while Trent and Carlos track down her attacker. "Lost and Found" - Gotta love a camping "bottle" episode, though it's sad they needed it with such a short run. Alex and Carlos agree to take a group of city kids camping, but end up picking a campsite near a militia group's headquarters. The group, calling themselves the Freedom Fighters, are planning an attack to steal $100 million dollars. Alex and another girl Danielle end up captured and Carlos and Walker are forced to rescue them. Trent, Kim and Butch focus on the b-story of fidning Danielle's missing father. They locate him safely and rescue him from a kidnapper who was also a heroine kingpin.

"Thunder by Your Side" - The series finale sees Trent and Carlos hired to work for the bad guy, though they don't know it at the time. Mr. LoPiato hired them to find a woman, Donna, only telling them that she stole $1.8 million from him. What they find out while on the case is that LoPiato is a gangster and Donna has information about his operations. He really wants to find and kill her. Lopiato then kidnaps Kim to force Carlos and Trent to turn over Donna and his money. Walker shows up in the third act to help rescue Kim and take down LoPiato.

The series was picked up to run on TV between the sixth and seventh season of *Walker, Texas Ranger*, in that show's time slot. During it's six-week run, it received a higher rating than *Walker* received in either of the seasons that bookended the show, but CBS chose not to move forward with a full season and, of course, passed on a second season.

The series was well written and enjoyable, I even watched the two episodes that Walker wasn't in. It was well acted and had decent fight scenes. Admittedly, I was a fan of *Walker* back in the day, though I haven't seen it since it went off the air, but I'd never heard of this series before this project came along. I definitely would have enjoyed seeing this go for a couple seasons andCBS dropped the ball on that. My favorite part was Alan Autry's portrayal of Butch, the bar owner/retired cop and landlord for the detective angency. I loved him as "Bubba" on *In the Heat of the Night*, so seeing him pop up here was a pleasant surprise. I purposely looked up nothing about the show prior to watching it, so I was surprised to see him appear. Marco Sanchez played Carlos Sandoval and ended up being in sixteen episodes of *Walker*, while James Wicek, who played Trent Malloy, appeared in thirteen episodes all from 1997-99.

–Dave Herndon

Martial Law (2000)

In this attempt to add a little rub from the far more popular *Walker, Texas Ranger*, a Chuck Norris sighting occurred in the sixteenth episode of season two entitled "Honor Among Strangers." Opening with a bank robbery for Sammo Law (martial arts veteran Sammo Hung) and team to foil, the episode starts with a bang. Law jumps off a pedestrian bridge, onto a van, does a summersault and flips a robber over his head to the ground all in one move. Then he spins away from the open van door, avoiding gunfire and kicks the door shut on a machine gun, foiling that bad guy as well.

Parker then shoots out the windshield of the van, before taking cover behind a mailbox to avoid being shot at. Law hides behind a thin tree to avoid more gunfire himself. The van and driver escape, though. The bank robbers, a militia named the Freedom Brigade, are talking in the next scene about losing one of their men. That's when Eagleton reveals that he's killed a Texas Ranger before, After the regular *Martial Law* cast talks with a military intelligence agent, they discover that Eagleton is an ex-military man who is now anti-government and looking to start a war. The weapons the bad guys used were supposed to have been destroyed by the local military base. With that sense of danger, back up was necessary and Ranger Walker makes an appearance. He mentions that he has approval to be in L.A. to look for the killer of his fellow Ranger. Chen is sthen ent undercover to the base to investigate. The Chuck Norris tie-in, lasting only a few seconds, was an excuse to get some of the Martial Law characters on the much more popular Walker, Texas Ranger, episode where the Eagleton storyline wrapped up in season eighteen's "Day of Cleansing." For martial arts aficionados, pairing Norris and Hung would be a special treat, but the link between narratives was a tenuous one. Hung made the similar small appearance on *Walker* to give Cordell some info on Eagleton, like Walker had done on *Martial Law,* making Eagleton the only character who is essential to both episodes. Norris appeared for a few seconds and was credited with a "Special Appearance By" title card. As could be expected, the ratings for *Martial Law* were waning at the time, and the series ended up being cancelled just a few months after the crossover. Nyby, the director, was also brought over from Walker, likely because Norris preferred working with his normal crew, even for the short appearance.

The best part of Norris' appearance on *Martial Law* is that when he first shows up he is asked "Who the hell are you?" and when Chuck responds with, "My name is Walker, I'm a Texas Ranger," the hook for the *Walker* theme song plays under his response. The Norris team can never be faulted for their consistent branding. Even for the early 2000s, the dialogue still resonates today (and also ties into that Norris branding). Ranger Walker sees fit to give Mr. Law some advice with the following sage wisdom, "Well Sammo, the Lone Ranger wore a mask, I wear a beard."

–Dave Herndon

The President's Man (2000)

As we open on this obviously made-for-TV movie, I am overcome with a desire to buy a rusty pickup truck, wrap myself in clothing in the style of the American Flag, drink a generic domestic light beer, and fire off two or three thousand rounds of ammunition. However, I master this impulse and trudge on past the screaming eagle opener.

The premise of this movie is simple. Every President of the United States since Lincoln has had a "man". Someone that only the President themselves know about. This "man" is the person that is called upon to do jobs that apparently SEAL Teams, nor Black Ops units are able to complete. The President, however, doesn't even know this person, they deal with them through an intermediary. Seems like a really bad way to keep something like this secret.

We first see our hero Chuck Norris as a college professor. Not sure what his subject is, but he has brought a katana to class to discuss the Way of the Samurai, and apparently to threaten his students.Though he just takes out his aggression on a defenseless apple. I do want to take a pause here to say that I believe Chuck Norris truly honors Japanese culture as opposed to appropriating it like other actors… This is absolutely shown during the completely unnecessary but still wonderful tea ceremony.

The hero's tea ceremony is cut short by the arrival of his Presidential Intermediary to tell him it is time to go to work. The First Lady has been taken hostage in Rio de Janeiro by a rebel group seeking an arsenal to achieve their goals. However, the President's Man shows up in his B-2 Stealth Bomber to parachute down to the roof of the hotel (with a quick pass by Christ the Redeemer) as noisily as he possibly can. Why these kidnappers decided to go fight as opposed to kill the hostage that they inexplicably were holding a knife to the throat of is beyond me.

A single grazing knife wound is sustained by Norris in the fight, and he base jumps out of the hotel with the First Lady strapped to him. As they reach the ocean, he appears to have tired of her company and cuts her free to fall into the water where some commandos that aren't supposed to know this Man exists are waiting. Remind me how this "man" is supposed to be such a well-kept secret?

The knife wound seems to be the last straw, and Norris goes to visit his predecessor (seriously how many people know about this extremely secret person that only the President is supposed to know about) to discuss retirement. Just a note, his predecessor looks younger than Norris does so how early on did this "man" retire? Regardless, the President's Man can't retire until they pick and train a successor.

At this point, I am going to step out of the movie plot and really just talk about the fact that this movie absolutely illustrates to me that there is no way that the United States government could be involved in the number of conspiracies that so many people believe they are. The only way to keep a secret is to tell NO ONE. There is not a punishment in the world that someone isn't going to risk at some point in time to make a quick buck. If someone had proof that we were hiding aliens in a bunker in Nevada, TMZ would make that person very, very, very, rich. Rich enough and famous enough that even if the government wanted to silence them, the act of silencing them would create more havoc than the person's whistleblowing. Now back to our regularly scheduled plot.

The next scene introduces us to the obvious choice to be the next President's Man. A covert operator with a bad attitude and no respect for the chain of command. Although, him punching out his Lieutenant is done to ensure his whole team is able to evacuate the Columbian drug den that they had just blown up so maybe it was a good thing. The Court Marshal did not see it that way, though, and sent him to prison.

After murdering someone, in self-defense, he comes to the attention of Chuck and magically they spring him just by the President's Man's secretary showing up at the prison. This alone doesn't seem to impress our potential replacement and definitely doesn't reduce his cocky attitude. We are then treated to a first for me. A training montage set to country music. This is made even more fun by the fact that the secretary is apparently an incredible martial artist and kicks Mr. Cocky's ass a few times over during the montage.

When a new mission comes in, our replacement "man" feels that he is ready for a solo mission to prove what he can do. His inability to follow a simple mission plan gets him and the person he is trying to rescue surrounded by the bad guys only to be rescued by a super flying kick from Chuck. This seems to finally humble our replacement "man" but only a little.

The final battle takes place back in the new hideout of the same Columbian Cartel that introduced us to our new hero. Only this time, it's personal. Teaming up with our Columbian drug lords is none other than the former military officer that killed Chuck's wife years ago. This man gets the ass-kicking of a lifetime by the hidden fist behind Chuck's beard while the new "man" is tasked with rescuing the nuclear physicist tasked with making the cartel a dirty bomb or see his family murdered in front of him.

As usual, Chuck Norris is victorious. I mean, if he hadn't the world would have literally stopped spinning. He has also found the new President's Man so he can ride off into the sunset having achieved his vengeance in the most Chuck Norris way possible.

–Pat Kawula

The President's Man: A Line in the Sand (2002)

If the opening to a Chuck Norris made-for-TV movie doesn't get your patriotic juices flowing, I don't think anything will. From the screech of the eagle to the close up on the eagle eye, on to the slow wipe to reveal a flapping flag of the United States of America, this just screams MURICA!

Just like the first movie in the *President's Man* series, we open right into the action. This time with the replacement "Man" in the field and Chuck and his TV daughter, Que, supporting him remotely with technology that would make the NSA jealous in 2002. Except, the interface looks like it's from 1950. As the Man is trying to escape, Que is constantly nagging him over their comms and making it that much more difficult for our young hero to concentrate on the task at hand. This exchange is the clunkiest version of flirting I have ever seen…

I am assuming some tragic accidents have occurred since we last saw the Man killing Columbian drug lords as he seems to have had extensive plastic surgery. Surgery that no one seems to be talking about, so I have to assume it is a sensitive subject. Maybe he didn't like the way he looked? Or it could be their attempt to hide his identity. If he looks different every time people see him on a mission, they may assume he is a new person!

We are introduced to a new POTUS in the next scene, and I was left scratching my head as to how I know the actor. Pulling up the actor's IMDb barely helped. The "known for" section didn't help as nothing jumped out at me as the source of memories. So, as I scrolled through the filmography of Mr. Robert Urich, I finally found a show that brought back memories of watching it with my mom and dad as a kid, *Spencer: For Hire*. THIS is the amazing thing of even the most obscure movie, there can always be something that might trigger a powerful memory. *Spencer:*

For Hire was one of those shows that our family always tried to be home to see. For those that are too young to know, back in the dark ages of the 1980s and 1990s, if you missed an episode of your favorite show, there was no Netflix, Hulu, or OnDemand to catch up. When you missed an episode you had to hope it would be one that would be re-run in the summer time when all the shows were shut down.

Anyway, back to the Man. Apparently his training is still not complete as we get another training montage in the sequel. This time, Chuck and Que seem to want our hero to train to challenge Neo from *The Matrix* to a bullet dodging battle. I think the Man may have a slight advantage as he is being taught to dodge those bullets blindfolded. Que seems to be getting a bit too much enjoyment out of pelting the Man with the practice balls, and even talks about the fact that she made sure to buy balls that would hurt more. Que seems to be trying really hard to make like she has no feelings for the Man, which usually means there is more to it than that.

I continue to question why exactly Chuck retired from being the Man, as most times when you choose your successor and retire, you stop doing the job you had been doing previously. Chuck seems like he just can't let go. Even more, he seems to want to take his daughter's job as he is providing as much support and information as she had previously. Maybe Chuck should start his own super-secret completely disavowed position called the President's Man's Man. He would get to be the guy the Man calls when the Man can't get the job done. Maybe even this time, the position could actually be secret.

Speaking of secrets, I know I spoke briefly about this in my essay about the first movie, but this position seems to be entirely odd in the way the secret is kept. After a particularly difficult mission, where no one was supposed to be allowed to do anything, the President's Chief of Staff gets a but suspicious. He confronts the President asking how anyone could have achieved this goal and that he had checked with all 46 possible organizations that could have completed the objective only to find out that none of them had done the job. The Chief of Staff is stonewalled by the President, and I honestly thought we were going to find out the Chief of Staff was behind the evil things going on, but it was not so.

The difficulty I have with this situation is that at least ONE of the 46 organizations had to be involved in some manner because the completion of the kidnapping mission was contingent on the Man and his detainee parachuting out of the hot zone and meeting a boat full of commandos a few hundred yards into a nearby body of water and hitching a ride on a Navy aircraft carrier. Just how many people are involved in this "secret"?

Based on the plot of this movie, I am a bit surprised at the release date. The overall plot is about a terrorist organization plotting a dirty bomb attack on the United States. This movie releasing less than a year after the events of 9/11, involving terrorists from the Middle East, and planning a nuclear attack on U.S. soil seems a bit risqué. Considering the number of plots that were scrapped, movies and episodes of TV shows that were delayed significantly, I can only assume this movie was not received well when it first aired. It also occurs to me that they kind of rehashed the first movie plot but changed it from Columbians to Arabs which seems even MORE offensive. Thankfully, Chuck and his protégé were there to save us.

–Pat Kawula

The Bells of Innocence (2003)

Jet was an Australian rock band that debuted in 2003 with an album titled *Get Born* featuring the hit song "Are You Going to be My Girl." Their 2006 follow-up album was titled *Shine On*, and while reviews of the album were mixed, one in particular was absolutely damning. *Pitchfork*, the holier-than-thou hipster music review site, gave the album a rating of a zero and the review of the album was nothing more than a video clip of a chimpanzee drinking its own urine.

The Bells of Innocence is a 2003 Christian family film co-written by Chuck Norris' son Mike and was directed by Alin Bijan. A Pitchfork-style zero rating with the chimpanzee clip is definitely tempting for this review, but it'd be a complete cop-out. *The Bells of Innocence* is nothing more than a harebrained attempt at blending *The Twilight Zone* with the pseudo-Christian ramblings of a scummy televangelist.

The basic premise of *The Bells of Innocence* is that three friends Jux (Mike Norris), Oren (Carey Scott) and Conrad (David A.R. White) decide to fly from Texas to Mexico for a church mission but make an emergency landing when their plane malfunctions. Jux, Oren, and Conrad stumble upon a small Texas town to seek help, but the inhabitants are under the possession of Satan. This would be a good foundation for a movie if it were in good hands, but the creative forces behind *The Bells of Innocence* just couldn't get their act together to deliver a solid film. Hell, this isn't even a mediocre film. It's downright awful.

Jux is the tough guy of the group and he's a recently divorced father who watched his daughter get killed while riding her bike. The whole flashback scene for that was so poorly developed that it ended up being unintentionally funny. Jux is having a Christopher Walken in *The Deer Hunter* kind of life sponsored by Bud Light. Conrad's thelevel-headed member of the group who's a holy-roller that's determined to go to

Mexico to deliver Bibles. Someone should have informed him that Mexico is overwhelmingly Christian, so good luck preaching to the converted, Conrad. Then there is Oren, who serves as the comedic relief for the film.

When the three main characters fly to Mexico, there is a mechanical failure and they land in the Texas desert. Tired, thirsty, and hot from wandering the desert, the three find refuge in a small Texas town where the locals are in some sort of trance. Phones are not available, plus nobody wants to help the three men. Matthew (Chuck Norris) is a somewhat helpful resident who tells them where they can find a radio to call for help. The radio is at some lady's house, but it malfunctions and their attempt at contacting their families falls short. The same lady owns a car, but there is some totally absurd reason that they can't leave town.

Jux, Oren, and Conrad discover that the town's inhabitants have been enslaved by Satan and once a year some kid in town has to be sacrificed because Satan deemed it necessary. After what seems to be an eternity, Matthew informs Jux, Oren, and Conrad that they are the chosen ones to stop the madness and must go into hero mode to save the day. In case you're wondering, the town they are stuck in is not Trope City. However, this is just the tip of the iceberg when it comes to the faults of this movie.

The Bells of Innocence opens sometime in the 1930's in Texas with a Native American grandfather and grandson building a fire. Some frantic white guy finds them and asks for help. A mob wearing robes carrying torches wants to kill the man, so the grandfather tells the grandson to find shelter. Both the man and grandfather are killed by the mob. The grandson is later seen in Jux, Oren, and Conrad's hometown during the present day as some crazy old man yelling random stuff, but his character really doesn't do anything for the overall plot of the film.

Even the role of the main villain is a bit confusing. There's a guy named Emeritus (Grant James) who seems to be the guy who has the town under his control, but there's this kid named Lyric (Gabby Di Ciolli) and she reminds Jux of his dead daughter. Yeah, totally shocking. Although she is nice to Jux, she seems to be working for or with Emeritus on some grand scheme for Satan. Then we meet Joshua (Marshall R. Teague) who is the mayor, and it isn't clear where he ranks on the town's villain chart. We soon discover that the robe wearing mob at the beginning of the movie are the inhabitants of the town. Also, there might be satanic zombies in town.

What's perhaps the most puzzling of all is Chuck Norris' character of Matthew. He's not that helpful when it comes to aiding the main characters, plus he later reveals himself as some angel watcher. We see he has powers to single handedly defeat Emeritus, Joshua, and their minions, but doesn't because of some cockamamie 'God has a plan' rule. So, God's going to let Satan run free and let his goons sacrifice kids for kicks? Brilliant. Where's that damn chimpanzee clip?

Even the Bible delivery mission that Jux, Oren, and Conrad undertakes is a colossal waste of time. Those dummies could have shipped them via UPS or FedEx and called it a day. One could bet dollars to donuts that the Bibles they are delivering are in English and not Spanish.

The final battle where Jux, Oren, and Conrad takes on the town Satan built is underwhelming. It should be no surprise their faith in God saves the day, but an odd plot twist is thrown in and it works as well as a McDonald's ice cream machine. *The Bells of Innocence* is the *Shine On* of cinema.

–Tony Doug Wright

Yes, Dear (2004)

Yes, Dear was an early 2000s sitcom about two sets of parents and their opposing ideas of how to parent their children and live their lives with Norris appearing in the Season Four, Episode Nine entry entitled "Jimmy and Chuck."

Jimmy, a security guard for a movie studio, is tasked with showing Chuck Norris how to be a security guard. This leads to ironic humor since Jimmy is barely a security guard himself. This episode is designed around Chuck Norris. There are dream sequences where a cast member appears with Chuck in some sort of movie or commercial. We get a parody of a Vietnam war movie, one where they poke fun at his exercise infomercials, and of course his Walker, Texas Ranger show. We are treated early on to a rendition of the theme to Walker, which is barely sung, but the audience laughed anyway. Jimmy quickly learns that the Chuck Norris he wants to spend time with, is only fictional. The real Chuck Norris is a family man, who plays with his kids and takes his acting job seriously. This is how to take a persona and have fun with it. Jimmy eventually breaks down and admits to Chuck that he thought spending time with him would be a lot more fun and Chuck explains that his films aren't real, however, it ends with a bar fight, just to show that Chuck still has moves and probably to show that it is him doing those moves.

When it comes to a role like this, no acting is required. Chuck plays himself and he is in on the jokes. There is a scene where Jimmy tells Chuck that being a security guard is dangerous work. Chuck listens to what Jimmy has to say, before he asks Chuck if he knows the words to little bunny foo-foo. Jimmy is taken aback. Chuck pokes fun at his infomercials by having an obese man do the infomercial with him and Chuck treats him just like everyone else, which is why the joke works so well. There are no big emotional scenes, nothing to test his action range, he showed up, had fun with the cast, and had some laughs.

Most of the humor comes from Jimmy realizing that his hero is a normal guy. Chuck has Jimmy listen to his kids playing and sets up a balloon to play with his kids in. I feel like Chuck did this show, just to make fun of himself and to not take himself too seriously. The actors are respectful to him, and they even acknowledge that stars get pestered with people wanting autographs and pictures with them, when, really, they just want to be left alone and do the work. It was a different side to Chuck Norris. It was one that he doesn't show a lot of. It could have been a real cathartic moment and to have an entire episode designed around your body of work, your persona, your family life, and your skill set, I am sure Chuck felt honored.

–Stephen Kessen

Dodgeball: A True Underdog Story (2004)

Who doesn't love an underdog story? The 2004 Red Sox. The 1980 US Men's Olympic Hockey Team (Do you believe in miracles? YES!). Appalachian State when they beat the University of Michigan. The list goes on. If you are a fan of NCAA Basketball, you probably know these underdogs as Cinderella. There is something ingrained in us to root for the person, team, or organization that isn't supposed to win. It makes us feel hopeful that someday even we can overcome our biggest obstacles.

However, *Dodgeball: A True Underdog Story* takes that to a new level. We meet our lovable band of losers at Average Joe's Gym. But are they really the lovable losers we think they are? While we may love Justin, Steve the Pirate, and the rest, Average Joe's is an obvious front for criminal activity. Average Joe's has about four members and is obviously not being supported by the money flowing in from them. It has always made me wonder which activities La Fleur (I mean even his NAME sounds shady) is actually using to stay afloat.

The theory that has always stuck out to me is that La Fleur is actually dealing steroids to Globo Gym. I mean, everyone over there is jacked to the extreme, even Ben Stiller looks swole. So, this story is actually about a client that stiffed his dealer. Kate is actually working at the bank to launder the money for the two of them. Now "The Flower" has overextended himself and can't make his payments back to the bank, and Kate is panicking on how to hide this all from her bosses, while White puts on a show like he bought La Fleur's debt from the bank.

Thankfully, this crazy dodgeball tournament scheme falls in all of their laps. Peter cons his crew into playing for his gym to save it. They are terrible and will be seeded as such. White then creates a team of ringers to ensure top seeding and also ensuring he and Peter can only meet in the finals. It's a bold move Cotton, let's see if it pays off.

Like true underdogs, the Average Joe's team is easily manipulated through anger, jealousy, and the desire to help someone they think is a friend. Additionally, once they are seeded, Average Joe's adds Kate, the dodgeball phenom to play way above their actually ability. She is there to ensure Average Joe's makes it to the finals, no matter what.

As we approach the finals, White comes into money and attempts to pay off La Fleur. However, La Fleur sees this as an opportunity to make even MORE money and screw over Goodman for daring to not pay him. He puts a huge bet on the underdogs then disappears to make Goodman become overconfident. La Fleur intentionally arrives late, knowing that the rules will allow for the three-judge committee to allow them to play even after technically forfeiting, thus increasing White's overconfidence. La Fleur is confident he can convince at least one of the officials to vote in his favor, knowing that Chuck Norris, the Patron Saint of the Underdog, is sitting on the panel and will absolutely vote for them to be allowed to play.

Kate knows that because Globo Gym and Average Joe's are in the finals, she does need to worry about which team wins, she will get paid no matter what. Thus, she lets down her guard and gets knocked out early without much emotion. If not for the little worm Justin finally playing well La Fleur's plan could have been wrecked completely. Justin's stalking of the head cheerleader at his school has finally paid off in multiple ways. First, he is able to impress the cheerleader by somehow knowing the entire routine the Cheer Team has to perform AND he is able to perform it perfectly in proper formation having never once practiced with the team. Oh man, I just realized. La Fleur must be Justin's Ritalin source! The matches before just never lasted long enough for it to kick in. That's why he was able to concentrate enough to perform well in the finals.

Speaking of sources, isn't it ironic that La Fleur disappears for a while and then Steve the Pirate comes out of what seems like a long-term hallucination where he thinks he is an actual pirate? I wonder what La Fleur was keeping Steve on? "The Flower" sure is more diabolical than he seems. He is approaching legitimate evil genius level in this plan. Every eventuality is being considered.

Once La Fleur wins the match, he rubs it in Goodman's face that not only did he realize Goodman was trying to screw him over, but also that he now has the capital to run the steroid ring himself. He doesn't need to use middlemen anymore. The bet La Fleur placed will fund all new Average Joe's locations all around the city, and thus opens up a huge new customer base. The marketing is brilliant, bring in the average folks trying to look like Hollywood action heroes and when they can't do it naturally get them hooked on the Juice! This runs Globo Gym out of town, and White Goodman has the same reaction any former steroid user has, massive weight gain. Kate obviously loves the criminal lifestyle and of course wants to be La Fleur's Queen.

The only person that seems to be legitimately as they appear is the patsy in this whole scheme, Gordon. Gordon thinks he is helping the place he loves get out of a terrible situation. Based on how Gordon gets when he is angry, I hope he never finds out the scheme La Fleur, Goodman, and the others are running. It will not be pretty if he does.

Speaking of people that won't be happy when they find out what La Fleur did, I am looking forward to the next installment in this movie franchise, *Dodgeball 2: Dodge Chuck Norris*.

–Pat Kawula

Walker, Texas Ranger: Trial by Fire (2005)

Four years after the final *Walker: Texas Ranger* episode aired in 2001, Walker and some of his old pals returned for a 2005 television movie. That was *Walker: Texas Ranger – Trial by Fire*. It was intended to be just the first in a series of such films, but the CBS executives at the time found the ratings wanting, and so the plans for future productions were scrapped. It is essentially a continuation of that very formulaic series. If you liked the show, you'll probably enjoy it. If you didn't, you'll find nothing new or challenging here.

The movie begins with Ranger Gage (Judson Mills) showing off his new car to Captain Cordell Walker (Chuck Norris). He is thrilled that it has a Hemi. Walker asks if he can drive it, with that "I'll show this asshole" look on his very scrutable face. You know where this is going from that moment on. He speeds and drives the car intentionally recklessly, with no thought to his being an officer of the law. Then a robbery is called in, and Walker does his best Steve McQueen *Bullitt* impression, driving against traffic and through barriers until Gage's car is completely totaled from ramming the getaway van at the scene of the robbery. After the collars have been made, Walker off-handedly says "Sorry about your car" to Gage, who shrugs it off.

So right away we are alerted not to expect too much here. Not that anybody probably was. The series seemed structured around (often unjustified) martial arts fight scenes, like every lawman and criminal in Texas has a black belt. There is less of that here to some degree, but more car chases and expensive action pieces abound throughout. Clearly the budget was larger than they were given for the episodic series. It all plays a bit more like a police procedural than it ever did as a series. Beautiful Janine Turner (so memorable in *Northern Exposure*) has joined the team as forensics expert Kay Austin. Her scenes take a cue from other police procedurals, like *NCIS* and *Law and Order*. She sees nifty animated graphics when she examines forensic evidence, which we assume are depictions of her mind at work.

Absent is Clarence Gilyard as James Trivette. He is replaced here by Andre Kristoff as Ranger Rhett Harper, who we learn used to play professional baseball. Trivette, of course, was once a Dallas Cowboy. Also, Salena Gomez, so good in *Only Murders in the Building*, shows up in a minor cameo.

The plot is a two-pronged one, and it leaves the door open for a future sequel that never came.

A new missile guidance system is stolen from a defense plant and winds up (accidentally) in a single father's briefcase. His thirteen-year-old son gets his hands on it and takes it to his tech savvy buddy to figure out what it is. Meanwhile, three Korean assassins show up, kill his father and and trash the house. Now the boy is missing and Walker and his team must find him before the Koreans do.

Meanwhile, a woman is murdered and all evidence points to Ranger Harper. Austin and Walker believe him when he says it's a setup, but they have to be able to prove it. Harper is booked into custody. Assistant DA Alex - Mrs. Cordell Walker (Sheree J. Wilson) - investigates Harper's case with Garrett Evans, who is Harper's partner.

Eventually the Koreans are all killed and the missile guidance system returned. The framing of Ranger Harper now comes front and center for the big wrap-up. It all comes to a head at Ranger Harper's murder trial. It is revealed that Evans was the real killer. He committed murder to set up Harper as revenge for his sister's suicide years earlier. And - in the film's most reality-bending, clunky old potboiler of a plot point - Evans grabs the bailiff's gun and holds him hostage to make an escape. But Harper will have none of that. He decks Evans, and goodness prevails.

Or does it? Just when you thought everything was wrapped up, the bank robber from the opening returns for a *Dirty Mary, Crazy Larry*-style, out of the blue, kind of left field ending. Angry at Harper for killing his son in the opening robbery scene, he comes gunning, in a crowded public place. It seems a lot of people want revenge on Harper, all at the same time. The bad guy is taken out after a short gun fight ensues. Alex finds, when the smoke has cleared, that she has been shot in the chest. She falls in the striped corridor as the camera cranes up, rotating, turning the floor stripes into animated, Saul Bass-like graphics. It's a neat shot. But we will never know if Alex lived or died.

For me, the best scenes are when the three Korean assassins show up. They are forces of nature, wildly kinetic human storms, knocking down everything in their paths. In one scene, one of them even dodges slow-motion bullets, ala *The Matrix*. They are right out of a Hong Kong action film from the 1990s. That said, they are woefully out of place with the tired and tame police drama that surrounds it. Also, some will find the treatment of the Koreans here to be more than a tad racist. They are mindless killing machines who do their work gleefully.

When all was said and done, I can't say *Walker: Texas Ranger – Trial by Fire* is an awful movie. It is slickly produced and competently played. It just felt so very familiar. Some may take comfort in watching the same plot points and the same character arcs over and over. They are familiar, and therefore perhaps, a safe and comforting background to our daily lives. For me, however, life is far too short to nickel and dime pieces of it away to this kind of dreary retread. As they say, it is time I will never get back.

–Ron Ford

The Cutter (2005)

The great pity of *The Cutter* is that there is at least the germ of a pretty good movie buried in here beneath all the clutter. One with a unique plot, that leaves much room for the examination of ethical behavior. It is a movie, however that would not have included the character Chuck Norris plays. It would instead have placed the titular figure – a diamond cutter in his eighties, an Auschwitz survivor – in the central position, and had the plot revolve around him.

The plot points involving the former cop-turned-private-eye, tough-guy-with-ethics John Shepard (Chuck Norris) feel phony, like they were tacked on after the script was written, in order to sell it as a Norris vehicle. It feels artistically false and structurally unnecessary.

The film, however, was shot in Spokane, Washington, where I currently reside. However, I know many of the people who were involved in the making of *The Cutter*. I interviewed several of them in the preparation of this piece. Their input made me come to have more respect for Chuck Norris, the man, than I had anticipated. While the Norris "brand" undoubtedly is misogynistic, chest-pounding, mediocre, cookie-cutter, and egotistical, the man himself, one-on-one, seems not to be. Which is in sharp contrast to my take-away of Steven Seagal, the subject of our previous volume.

The plot involves the theft of an ancient breastplate, referred to in Jewish scriptures, along with a priceless, uncut diamond of incomparable quality. The stone winds up in Spokane, Washington, where it is hoped that retired cutter Isaac Teller (Bernie Kopell of *Love Boat* fame in a very respectable performance), who developed a legendary, but technically difficult, cut while carving up stones for the Nazis at Auschwitz. However, it isn't long before Teller figures out that he is being used. He refuses to do his famous cut anymore, since its technique was developed under unspeakable duress.

So, the bad guys go after his daughter (Joanna Pacula), in order to coerce the old man into doing their bidding. Well, things in the end don't go well for the bad guys, and there is some action and stuff.

Oh, yeah, and Chuck Norris shows up once in a while as ex-cop P.I. John Shepard to question people, and to get into some fights.

On the upside, the film makes a convincing argument for Eastern Washington as a versatile movie location. The opening scenes in the desert, depicting the theft of the breastplate and stone, were created convincingly on the prairies west of Spokane. And the city itself has seldom been showcased to better effect on film.

If only its storytelling were as committed and polished as its look.

When Chuck Norris comes to your town, the rumors fly thick and fast. At the time it was shooting, the scuttlebutt was that Norris was aloof and impersonal on the set, and that he was constantly surrounded by bodyguards. But actor Jhon Goodwin, who played an FBI agent in the film, told me that was far from accurate.

"He had an assistant, as most [movie stars} do," Goodwin said. "He [the assistant] was a heck of a nice guy, as well. My impression was that he knew what he was doing, and could handle himself in a situation, if he had to. I mean, if you're Chuck Norris, think of the knuckleheads that's going to attract."

To a person, nobody had anything bad to say about interactions with Norris, except for one actor who said Norris – sixty-five years old at the time – had hair and teeth that looked like they were painted on, like he "could have been in *What Dreams May Come* and saved the special-effects budget."

The most resounding endorsement of the man they call Norris, however, came from Jason Payne, the young editor of the film. The cutter of *The Cutter*, if you will. He worked as an editor at Spokane's North By Northwest Productions at the time, and the Norris film was his first feature assignment. The pressure to succeed was heavy on the young editor.

"About a week into filming, they shot the big climactic fight between Chuck and Daniel Bernhardt," Payne said. "Here I was, a twenty-five-year-old kid, actually getting the chance of a lifetime to edit a Chuck Norris fight scene." But after an initial pass at the scene, Payne was told Norris wanted to sit in on an editing session.

Gulp.

The next day, Payne answered a knock at the door of his editing suite and the cowboy-booted one strolled in with a warm smile and a firm handshake. "I was instantly put at ease," Payne said.

Norris was only interested in the cutting of the fight scene. Payne played the first rough cut he had of the scene. After it had played, Norris said, "Not too bad. There are some spots I'd like to go over with you, though. Play it again." Payne started it again, and a few seconds in, Norris said, "Okay, right there. That punch is a miss. You can't use that."

Payne went back and looked again, and sure enough, Norris was right.

"Chuck had spotted that in real time. I opened up the alternate takes and found a replacement."

Norris found other moments where he thought it was too obvious that his stunt double, Chip, was being used instead of himself, and a few other fine points.

"We worked together on the scene for nearly an hour, and I was in awe of the masterclass I was receiving [in editing action scenes]."

So, in conclusion, The Cutter is a movie with an intriguing premise that never comes together due to its lack of focus - dividing its running time between an inventive plot, and a dreary re-tread of action-move tropes performed by one of the genre's blandest leading men.

On the other hand, we learned that Norris seems to be a decent man who treats co-workers well and has a canny sense of his own screen persona, particularly in fight scenes.

–Ron Ford

The Expendables 2 (2012)

CONFIDENTIAL file_booker_lone_wolf EYES ONLY

init connection @server [redacted]

access folder [booker_lone_wolf]

override

run password crack

init login

\\ACKNOWLEDGE_RECEIPT

\\CONFIDENTIAL_FILE

Name: Arnold Bokanowski
Codename(s): Booker, "Lone Wolf", Lone Wolf Booker
DOB: March 10, 1940
Marital Status: UNKNOWN
Known Affiliations: The Expendables 2 (Russian Mine/Bulgaria)
Listed as: LONE MERCENARY

<u>DETAILS</u>

Early History:

Born Arnold Bokanowski to Peter (an art dealer) and Marianne (a music teacher) (nee Korè) Bokanowski. He attended Catholic schools in his hometown of Tipton, Kansas. Solitary by nature, Arnie (as called by former teachers and classmates) would not join in group play unless specifically invited or he saw a need to level the playing field. It was noted throughout various interviews, he chose to side with those he considered underdogs and outcasts even in ordinary peer play {see attachment *Bokanowski_Background*}.

Bokanowski attended Central Kansas University and graduated with a degree in Business Administration with an emphasis on Analytics and Project Management {see attachment *Bokanowski_CKU_Transcript*}. He joined the Marine-tracked Navy ROTC. Upon graduation and entry into the Marines, he made his intention known to enter the Scout Sniper Program.

Military Life

Bokanowski served [REDACTED] years in the Marines before retiring in [REDACTED].

Military Achievements

[REDACTED]

Military Posts

[REDACTED]

Firearms Proficiency

Per his elite training, Bokanowski is proficient is the M40 rifle, as well as all its variants, though his personal firearm is the Heckler & Koch G36KV. It is believed his personal arsenal has been collected through various shell companies and possibly with assistance with the CIA and other foreign intelligence agencies. He has within his domestic possession at least 75 separate firearms ranging from a [REDACTED] 9mm to [REDACTED] automatic grenade launcher. This inventory does not include overseas storehouses.

Civilian Life

According to multiple sources within Chicago's Chamber of Commerce, he is a principal, but silent, partner of the consulting firm, Wilder and Donigan, whose corporate one-sheet contains the single line, "It's done" {see attachment *Bokanowski_One_Sheet*}. Agency calls to the offices are routed to professional secretaries and the client list is confidential. All attempts to meet with either Bokanowski, Wilder, or Donigan have been met with outright refusals due to an unverifiable referral, and in the case of one persistent Agent, a blocked phone number and a personal visit from the FBI.

Bokanowski is described as amicable and soft spoken, and those who claim to have visited his brownstone in [REDACTED] describe his "meticulously manicured" backyard nestled along a deck he built himself, as well as a water feature with live koi. These same sources also say he is an avid woodworker, turning out several toys annually for local gift-giving charities. His home is "elegantly appointed". Within the Agency, it is believed he chooses to not mix socially. {see attachment *Bokanowski_Home*}.

This is at odds with reports of Bokanowski appearing at large social gatherings with a wife named Lucille or Hayden or Justine or Octavia. Of the sources interviewed for this report, none of his "wives'" names comes up twice. The descriptions of the various "hers" also vary from Italian-born, to American, to South African. They do not stand out in manner or dress or looks. They are always attractive, but not what would be described as "beautiful". they are conversational, but not chatty. They are unremarkable in every way, blending into the fuzzy past that is Bokanowski's background. It is believed actresses {see attachment *Bokanowski_Wives*} are hired by shell companies, given scripts and clothiers, transportation and lodging. What happens to them after their debut is unknown, but it is believed that they are given substantial amounts of money and new identities to move anywhere in the world. Bokanowski has never used the same wife twice and none in his social circle care to notice {see attachments, *Bokanowski_Personal*}.

He maintains an away home near the Troyan Monestary in Bulgaria. There are two standing structures on the property inside of a 3-meter stone wall. He receives deliveries from the local grocery as well as local courier when in residence.

Life as Booker, "The Lone Wolf"

It is not known when Bokanowski became Booker, the Lone Wolf, or under what circumstances he was pressed into the private "consulting" business. It is known that he prefers to work alone and using his consulting company as a cover for communications with the CIA and other organizations, he travels extensively under untraceable identities. It is also known that for a period of [REDACTED], he worked exclusively in the protection of [REDACTED], a village in Bulgaria, investigating the disappearances and murders of its townsmen. It is believed he had been following a larger group of violent mercenaries, calling themselves The Sang, led by Jean Vilain. It is known The Sang were permanently disbanded in 2012.

Booker owns a Boston Dynamic military-grade robot, model SPOT. Housed in Bulgaria, it is used for surveillance of property, as well as short missions in and around the area. It may be responsible for the deaths of Agency operatives [REDACTED], however their fates remain unknown as their bodies have not been recovered. It is also believed he owns a legacy-model AlphaDog, at a tertiary homestead in [REDACTED]. It is not known the reasons behind the purchase of this property.

Due to Booker's success rate, he is not only sought after by government agencies, but also private citizens who can afford his consulting fees. Booker's wealth is unknown. He maintains multiple bank accounts in offshore banks controlled by multiple levels of shell companies.

Final Notes

If you are reading this document, Lone Wolf Booker already knows you have it. You will be the [{COUNT CURRENT+1} REDACTED] person to have accessed this file and the [{COUNT CURRENT+1} REDACTED] person to realize that Lone Wolf Booker does not exist.

This document serves as a historical record of inaccuracies and falsehoods.

Be warned that you cannot be warned. He already knows.

You are the [{COUNT CURRENT+1} REDACTED] person to

//end file

//delete file

–Montilee Stormer

The Goldbergs (2015)

The Chuck Norris is weak with this one, it's a tiny cameo that isn't even on screen.

Mr. Norris only appears as the voice of Chuck Norris reading a forged letter from C. Norris. It's the very last scene of the episode, which was one of the first in the series to not be primarily focused on the character of Adam Goldberg. This was season three, episode five and entitled "Boy Barry."

Norris' cameo was all in Barry's head, as Barry read the letter in Chuck's unique voice.

The best part is when Chuck said "douchenozzle" in the letter. The entire scene, including the set up with Chuck's voice in under 43 seconds long, in a 'sneeze and you'll miss it' cameo.

The scene shows Barry walk into the Goldberg house yelling at Adam, who was going through the mail.

Adam hands Barry the letter, who gets excited when he sees that it is from "C. Norris, 10202 W. Washington, Blvd., Hollywood, California. It was addressed to "Master Barry Goldberg."

As soon as Barry starts to "read" the letter, the viewer is treated to Chuck's voice instead of Barry's as the inner monologue. For your own mental gymnastics, try the following in the dulcid tones of Mr. Norris:

Dear Barry,

Sorry it took so long to write back, but thanks for the nice words and for being a fan. I've given a great deal of thought to what I'm about to tell you. Herein lies my most precious secret to being a true martial arts warrior...

If you have a brother, obey him. He has a power you do not yet understand.

Godspeed, douchnozzle.

Sincerely,

Chuck Norris

Barry's glee over the letter melted as he got through it, of course, obviously onto Adam's prank with the last line. When Adam asked what the letter said, and used douchenozzle, Barry angrily retorted, "It says I should kick your ass." Strangely, the douchenozzle line was edited out for syndication and re-runs, but the clip remains intact on various websites.

The cameo was the perfect amount of Chuck Norris for this series, which frequently referenced 80s popular culture. Barry had several times in the past mentioned his enjoyment of both Chuck's movies, and karate lifestyle, making it the perfect time to add the tag scene and get the man himself the role.

–Dave Herndon

Total Gym (2015)

I'm an oddball here. Of all of the writers in this book, I am the only one who has never seen a Chuck Norris movie. I've only seen one episode of *Walker*, which wasn't really by choice. You see, I had to spend a night in the hospital with a kidney infection back in 1999, and my only entertainment option was the CBS Saturday prime time lineup. There was the guy who was almost Cable running around with a magical newspaper and the actor who did brown face in *Short Circuit* followed by two hours of terribly choreographed martial arts, and for some reason, Arsenio Hall was there. If the people from Guinness had been in the room, I would have the world record for pressing the morphine button more times than every 1990s one hit alt-rock lead singer combined.

Still, I needed a way in. Someone had to cover Chuck's infomercials, and I decided to dive onto multiple grenades. Hell, nobody even mentioned the QVC video. I did that on my own. I still don't quite understand why. Trust me, you won't either.

Total Gym started in 1974, and two years later, its debut commercial and I were born. Twenty years after that, they recruited middle-aged Chuck Norris and Christie Brinkley to star in their first infomercial, while I was the assistant manager at an auto parts warehouse. There we were, three unsuspecting nobodies on a path that would lead us to converge in front of your eyeballs. Total Gym's YouTube channel is still very active, and there are approximately eight million videos to search through. I chose infomercials from around 2015. I wanted to see how 942 years of working out with this thing was going for Chuck and Christie.

In the first infomercial, we start out with a few testimonials. My favorite is from a woman who was in no way overweight, but she acts like she let herself balloon up to what appears to be 110 pounds. That's morbidly obese if you're a house cat. If you're a human being of average height, you're probably malnourished. Then Chuck shows up with his wife, and they work out on these ding dong contraptions in a room that is lined with kitchen cabinets for no discernable reason. I've never used a Total Gym, but it appears to be a more worthless version of a rowing machine. You pull on a cord while the pad you sit on slides on a track with what looks like zero resistance. I have no idea what this does. Chuck brags about men at the gym groping his biceps, which aren't really all that big. You're welcome for that unnerving image.

He even starts bragging about his kid using this thing. First of all, he's about ten. How is he not Chuck's great grandchild? Chuck sits there and says we should try to arm wrestle his kid. I'm no athlete, but I'm pretty sure I could kick this kid's ass. Actually, he should be about 20 right now, so never mind. Probably a bad idea. The funniest part of that segment is Chuck shaming everyone for sitting around and watching TV. Hey, genius, how do you think you're selling these things?

I haven't even started on Christie Brinkley. She pretty much says and does all of the same crap as the rest of the people in the testimonials, but there are two very specific differences. One exercise she does is basically her spreading her legs and thrusting her crotch at the camera. Another has her sliding back and forth on her knees while popping her butt in the air. I don't know what this does for her, but every straight Boomer guy watching immediately reminisces about their glory days, when you could sexually harass a woman, and she'd pretend to like it.

In the second infomercial, all of the testimonials are the same, Chuck drags his kid out again, and you get the same sales pitch. One thing they add is a group that will work out using only the Total Gym for three weeks so you can see the results. A crop of already mostly fit Canadians comes in with a professional trainer to try to reach their goals. SPOILER ALERT: They do it. Totally not rigged. Exactly like it would be for you at home.

We're already in too deep, so let's talk about the 2016 QVC appearance. It's weird. Some forty-something meathead with bleached hair bounds over to Chuck, who seems to have aged significantly in the very short time since the last infomercial. Yes, he's 76 at that point, but he looks odd. It's almost like someone peeled the skin off of Chuck Norris' skull and wore it as a mask. His hair has already looked like dried out shag carpeting for decades, and I can never figure out his beard. It doesn't look real. It looks like it's made out of the fuzz from the Masters of the Universe Mossman action figure. It upsets me.

This all combines into a confusing form. Is this the real Chuck? Is it a body double? Has Chuck entered the uncanny valley? I may never know. What I do know, thanks to this live unedited broadcast, is that the Total Gym does nothing. An old woman on set bounces around doing ten different exercises while having a full conversation, and not only does she not break a sweat, but her breathing never changes. Not for a single second.

Honestly, after watching over an hour of this, I can't expect that a workout consisting of turning yourself into a human yo-yo with a series of frat boy air humps is going to get anyone in shape. Maybe the Total Gym is total crap, but it doesn't hold a candle to Chuck's dry sales pitch. Thankfully, it folds up so you can easily slide it under your bed, which you'll do after using it twice, and that's where it will live for all of eternity.

–Kevin Moyers

Hawaii 5-0 (2020)

In a now-rare television appearance, Chuck appears as Sgt. Major Phillips in season ten, episode twenty-one entitled "A 'ohe ia e loa'a aku, he ulua kapapa no ka moana." The episode opens with Steve (Alex O'Loughlin) getting a letter from his mother who had died four months earlier. That letter was a cypher that was worth killing over. Near the end of the episode Danny was attacked by someone trying to steal that cypher. The bulk of the episode has them trying to track down a good samaritan who had helped a stranger. The crew figures out it is war hero Lincoln Cole (Lance Gross), who was on the island under an assumed name after going AWOL just days after winning a Purple Heart. That leads them to Sgt. Major Phillips (Norris), who had been the training officer for Cole when he started his military career on the island. Phillips attempts to lie to the officers to keep Cole hidden away, but eventually they chase him down through the woods and manage to take him into custody. While interviewing Cole, the team realizes he's wanted by some very bad men, and decide to help him take them down, all the while rescuing a woman and her child.

Originally set to be a two-hour series finale for the end of the show's tenth season, when COVID-19 hit, CBS chose to break up the two-hour block and run it as separate episodes. That means that Norris ended up in the penultimate episode, not the finale like producers had planned, but they were ok with it, after trying and failing to get him to make a guest appearance for several years. Norris agreed to the small role as a favor to series showrunner Peter M. Lenkov, but only had a tiny amount of screentime. This episode was his first on-screen role outside of infomercials since 2012's *The Expendables 2*, and first role of any kind since 2015's voiceover cameo on *The Goldbergs*. For a man who hadn't acted in about eight years, he did well with the role. At 80-years-old Norris is no longer an action star, but still did well standing against the series leads while arguing with them and trying to protect his former protege.

The scene ran about 45 seconds total and was all of Norris' time in the episode. It definitely left his fans wanting more of him but gave them a dose of Chuck they had wanted for years. Norris had retired from acting after *The Expendables* to take care for his ailing wife, making this brief cameo that much more special to his fans.

–Dave Herndon

The Norris Legacy

Flashback time.

It's 2005 and, aside from a silly non-sequitur cameo in *Dodgeball: A True Underdog Story*, it's been a decade since Chuck Norris' last theatrically released movie. Following the success of such '80s b-grade action flicks as *Invasion U.S.A.*, *Missing in Action*, and *Delta Force*, the '90s saw the martial artist's career decline into a mire of family-friendly "comedies" and exercise infomercials.

Now, in the early 2000s, Norris barely even qualifies as a D-list celebrity, notable only for the inexplicable continuation of *Walker, Texas Ranger*, a TV series which seems to exist solely to provide Conan O'Brien with regular joke material.

In other words, there is no good reason for a teenager in the year 2005 to give even the slightest shit about Chuck Norris. Yet there I am, at age 18, printing off Chuck Norris Facts in college. Later, my friends and I will take turns reading them aloud while laughing ourselves hoarse during one of the many aimless car rides we take instead of going to class.

"Chuck Norris doesn't sleep. He waits."

"Chuck Norris counted to infinity. Twice."

"Chuck Norris wasn't born. He shed a woman."

Unbeknownst to any of us at the time, Chuck Norris Facts were originally Vin Diesel Facts and started their life on the *Something Awful* message boards. At some point, the chrome-domed *Fast & the Furious* star was replaced by his ginger-bearded precursor and a Chuck Norris Fact Generator website was established, rescuing the aging action-movie also-ran from looming pop cultural obscurity and reinventing him as an Internet Age Paul Bunyan, a mythic figure capable of impossible feats.

"Chuck Norris can do a wheelie on a unicycle."

"Chuck Norris can watch *60 Minutes* in half an hour."

"Chuck Norris can strangle you with a cordless phone."

We weren't the only ones who had, seemingly out of nowhere, developed this bizarrely specific obsession with Chuck Norris-themed tall tales. For a brief window of time in the 2000s, Chuck Norris Facts were as ubiquitous as Livestrong bracelets and Crazy Frog ringtones, and ultimately they aged about as well.

It's difficult to answer even the simplest questions about the Chuck Norris Facts phenomenon without raising even more questions in the process. Why Chuck Norris instead of Vin Diesel? Well, because it's funnier that way. *Why* is it funnier? Hell, why is it funny *at all*? What exactly is the joke? Are we celebrating Chuck Norris or mocking him? In either case, *why*? What makes Chuck Norris worthy of our reverence or derision?

The answers to those questions will change depending on who you ask. One suspects that the initial intent was indeed to mock, which is why Diesel was quickly replaced with Norris. It is, after all, easier to derive humor from the inflated ego of a washed-up action star than that of a currently successful one.

Still, why Chuck Norris and not, say, his infinitely more absurd peer Steven Seagal? The reasoning may be that Seagal's cartoonish eccentricities leave little room for embellishment; he's already such a bizarre character, while Norris is relatively bland. Arguably, Norris represents such an utter dearth of personality and charisma that, outside of having a beard, the only identifying feature most modern audiences would know him for is the perceived masculinity inherent in a filmography built on gunfire, explosions, roundhouse kicks, and little else.

That's why the focal point of hyperbole for nearly all Chuck Norris Facts is masculinity—more specifically toxic masculinity, as evidenced by the repeating themes of stoicism, violence, and sexual virility.

"Chuck Norris' tears could cure cancer. Too bad he never cries."

"Chuck Norris threw a grenade and killed 50 people. Then the grenade exploded."

"Chuck Norris visited the Virgin Islands. They are now known as the Islands."

As with any form of spoof or satire, though, there are no shortage of people who fail to grasp the intended sarcasm. That's where the question of mockery versus celebration comes in.

Whether meant as a gentle ribbing towards Norris or a mean-spirited skewering, obvious at least is that part of the humor is supposed to come from not simply the outsized exaggeration of toxic masculinity, but from the tongue-in-cheek veneration of it. Divorced of this context, Chuck Norris Facts become a mechanism for *earnestly* celebrating traits that were meant to be celebrated *ironically*, i.e., traits that were faux-celebrated because the intended joke was that *these are not traits worthy of celebration.*

In any case, one can hardly imagine Norris lucking into a better PR jackpot so late into his career. These days, Norris is probably better known as a meme than for any of his martial arts championships or film roles. It can be easy to forget that there's an actual person behind the punchline, and it can be even easier to overlook the caliber of that person.

Here, then, are some *real* Chuck Norris Facts:

Chuck Norris opposed the Boy Scouts of America lifting their long-held ban against gay members.

Chuck Norris believes that the U.S. government is poisoning its citizens with chemtrails and vaccines.

Chuck Norris warned that Barack Obama's presidency would usher in "a thousand years of darkness."

(Yes, he really said that.)

In many ways, the real Chuck Norris is just as ridiculous and hilarious a figure as Chuck Norris Facts would have us believe, only much less epic and much more pathetic. This is a man so small, so insecure in his own manhood, and so afraid of the world around him that that the mere idea of people having different sexual preferences, receiving basic immunization shots, or voting for a black president fills him with apocalyptic terror.

It's a far cry from the silver screen action-hero who took on literal armies without breaking a sweat, and an even farther cry from the god-among-men who supposedly threw a roundhouse kick so hard that it broke the speed of light, went back in time, and accidentally wiped out the dinosaurs. In his films and in his "facts," Chuck Norris is often the hero. In real life, he's not even close.

For those who view Chuck Norris Facts through a lens of toxic masculinity—a lens of racism, misogyny, homophobia, anti-intellectualism, and preening moralism—one could not hope to find a more appropriate idol to worship.

For the rest of us, the fictional Norris is infinitely preferable to the factual one.

–William Tea

The Authors

Jon Arking *(aka Jon King)* is a Michigan-based broadcaster and journalist with over 35 years of experience. He has authored two children's books, *Ishkadoodle: A Boy, His Vacuum & Their Outerspace Adventure* and *Ishkadoodle & The 8 Planets of Hanukkah*. He is also the co-author of *Hot Mess* and the upcoming *Grounds*.

Hall CF Astell is a critic, author, publisher, and film festival director who runs the Apocalypse Later Empire from his lair in Phoenix, AZ. He has six books in print through Apocalypse Later Press. *Apocalypse Later Reviews* will celebrate its fifteenth anniversary in 2022. The Apocalypse Later International Fantastic Film Festival (ALIFFF) is in its sixth year. He brings quality films to new eyeballs at conventions across the southwest through the Apocalypse Later Roadshow. His website is apocalypselaterempire.com.

Daryl Bean lives, works, and does things in relative anonymity and is totally fine with that. He'd put his website address here, but he doesn't have one.

Kurt "Thunderlord" Belcher lives in the mythical kingdom of Kentucky. He must continually dodge Bloody Thraborlaxes and Golden Shlob Bœars to make his way to the market at Neckboneton to sell his ridiculous paper scribbles. He likes dogs.

John Bruske is a co-host to many podcasts, including the *Jean Pod Van Dammecast*, *Rage in a Cage*, and *Everyday I'm Russellin'*. When not trying to completely watch the Canon Films filmography, he spends time with his family and working on intellectual properties.

Michael Cieslak is a lifetime reader and writer of horror, mystery, and speculative fiction. He is an officer in the Great Lakes Association of Horror Writers and is the editor of the *Erie Tales* anthologies. His works have appeared in a number of collections including *DOA: Extreme Horror, Dead Science, Vicious Verses and Reanimated Rhymes*, the GLAHW anthologies, *Alter Egos* Vol 1., and the collaborative steampunk novel *Army of Brass*. *Urbane Decay*, a collection of Michael's short fiction, was released in 2018 by Source Point Press. Michael is the Editor in Chief of Dragon's Roost Press and his mental excreta, including his personal blog *They Napalmed My Shrubbery This Morning*, can be found on-line at thedragonsroost.net.

Paul Counelis is a freelance writer (*Rue Morgue, Scary Monsters, Fear Finder, Fright Times*), author (*Evil World Outside, 25 Underrated Horror Films and 'The Exorcist', The Greatest Horror Movie Ever Made*) and member of the Flint Horror Collective hailing from urban, renegade Flint, Michigan. As Uncle Salem he is the voice of horror punks LORDS OF OCTOBER and the host of a weekly online radio show, *Blank Generation with Uncle Salem*.

Jeff Dolniak is an enigma wrapped in a damp hanky. Over the past 45 years, Jeff has strived for mediocrity with acting roles in cult films such as *Blown, Desert Man Beast* and *Sportkill*. Cult film aficionados may also know him as the creator of the popular DVD series, *42nd Street Forever*. Currently he churns out news and reviews for Cinema Head Cheese.

Ron Ford is an actor, writer and filmmaker from the Seattle area. In 1994, after moving to LA, he sold his first screenplay, which became the horror hit, *The Fear.* He became a filmmaker in 1997 with his directorial debut, *Alien Force*, starring Burt Ward of Batman fame. He became a gun for hire for film distributors, who could be relied upon to deliver salable movies on budget and on schedule. He produced, wrote and directed more than a dozen genre titles, including *Hollywood Mortuary, Tiki, Mark of Dracula* and *Witchcraft XI: Sisters in Blood*. As an actor, he can be seen in the movies *Home of the Brave, Killer Tomatoes Eat France*, and many others, as well as on the TV shows *Z Nation, The Young Riders, Two Busy Debras* and *Hey, Dude.* In 2003 he moved to Spokane, WA where he continues to live and work.

David C. Hayes is an author, performer, filmmaker and academic. Visit him online at www.davidchayes.com.

Dave Herndon is a pretty simple man. He runs a newspaper in his day job, and does many creative things "on the side," in his spare time, including writing and editing comic books and stories, designing enamel pins and iron-on patches and much more. He owns the vending business Turtle Trinkets and generally just likes to enjoy life… and pizza!

Kent Hill is screenwriter, author, publisher and podcaster. First published in the United States in 2013 by StrangeHouse Books, Hill would go on to write numerous novellas and short stories published individually and in a variety of anthologies. He currently has screenplays in development and is a writer of upcoming films from Rene Perez at www.thedarkestmachines.com. He lives on 'The Downs' in Queensland, Australia with his wife and son.

Pat Kawula is a writer, editor, and curator of the award-winning comic anthology *Get in the Game* published by Source Point Press. When he is not hiding under his desk suffering from an incurable case of Imposter Syndrome, he will peek out to write something witty. This bio is NOT one of those times... although maybe it is. Who knows?

Stephen Kessen was born July of 1989 in Cincinnati Ohio. He recently earned his master's degree from Regent University with a focus on Directing and Producing. He writes screenplays, directs movies, and acts with his film *Moving Ashley* winning over a dozen awards from various festivals across the world. When he's not working in the performing arts, he can be found reading murder mystery novels, traveling, and playing with his two cats, Chloe and Tybalt.

Joshua "Samurai" Knode is a Do-goooder, Righter of Wrongs, Champion of the Little Guy, and all-around badass. He is the author of *Second Sun, Obsidian Road* and *True: A Gunslinger's Tale* and host of the podcast *Samurai Says*. He lives in Ohio with one cat, his brother and an embarrassingly large collection of vintage playing cards.

Joe LaLonde is an award-winning blogger who loves to combine his love for movies and his desire to see people grow their leadership abilities. He writes about leadership at https://jmlalonde.com and has released a book titled *Reel Leadership* which can be found wherever books are sold.

Corey Maslowski considers himself a connoisseur of terrible movies and TV series, and loves adding that charm and flair to his work. Born and raised in Northern Michigan, he is best known for his work on the story "Logging Out" in the comic anthology *Get in the Game* as well as pieces featured in the collection *Theater of the Mind.*

Kevin Moyers is an author and podcaster who feels fully vindicated in choosing Jean Claude Van Damme in the "Who would win a fight?" argument way back in the 1990s.

Andrew J. Rausch is a film journalist and the author of more than fifty books. This includes such titles as *The Cinematic Misadventures of Ed Wood* (w/ Charles E. Pratt Jr.), *The Films of Martin Scorsese and Robert De Niro*, and *My Best Friend's Birthday: The Making of a Quentin Tarantino Film*. He writes for numerous publications and is an online editor for *Diabolique* magazine. He lives with his wife and children in Independence, Kansas.

Jed Rowen is an actor living in Los Angeles who would rather not have a political discussion with Chuck Norris.

A P Sessler, a resident of North Carolina's Outer Banks, wishes he could stick to walls and jump trees without the aid of wires while fighting 50 bad guys at once. His all-time favorite martial arts film is the Shaw Brothers' *Five Elements Ninjas* aka *Chinese Super Ninjas.*

Kristina Stancil is an academic living in North Mississippi. Stancil is studying to be a criminologist. She has written one true crime book for the History Press, numerous short stories, and is formerly the managing editor of Blood Reign.Lit. She is a member of the American Crime Writers League and formerly a member of the Horror Writers Association.

Montilee Stormer is a horror writer, film reviewer, and podcaster who never expected to actually live the inescapable horror of a Steven Segal movie. She now silently weeps for what could have been, but feel free to Google her name and despair along with her.

William Tea doesn't know aikido, but he does know how to write scary stories, as well as the occasional cult film review. Stalk him online at williamtea.com.

Tony Doug Wright is a writer of comics and a graphic novel for Source Point Press. He's a husband, father, historian, lost soul of rock and roll, and a true crime writer.

www.ingramcontent.com/pod-product-compliance
Ingram Content Group UK Ltd.
Pitfield, Milton Keynes, MK11 3LW, UK
UKHW021912190726
13853UKWH00002B/641

9 798887 710181